MALICE
in
PINDERLAND

*A story of love and intrigue in Spanish Wells
and Harbour Island.*

Written by

DEREK HAWKINS

ISBN: 1-4107-0297-9 (e-book)
ISBN: 1-4107-0298-7 (Paperback)

This book is printed on acid free paper.

1stBooks – rev. 02/13/03

Dedication

*This book is dedicated to the people of Spanish Wells
who have been generous with their friendship and
unselfish in their acceptance of an outsider into their
community. To be able to call Spanish Wells home is a
privilege granted to just a select few.
I'm proud to be one of the few.*

CHAPTER ONE

The telephone rang for the third time in the past half an hour. Its persistent jangle was starting to bother me because it was a reminder to me that I could not continue to pretend that I was unavailable. I had a pretty good idea who was calling me and I had seriously considered not answering the infernal machine ever again, but I realized that if I continued to ignore it, I would never get any peace.

I glanced at my watch as I picked up the receiver; it was just a habit, for the time of the call was of no consequence, nor of any relevance to the day, month or year.

"Hello" I said without emotion.

There was a long silence as if the caller was surprised that he or she had finally received an answer. I remained silent. I had learned a long time ago that the less you had to say the more likely you were to avoid being trapped into divulging information that was best kept to yourself.

"It's Joe"

"I figured it would be you" I answered.

There was another long silence as each of us waited for the other party to continue the conversation.

"The boys are worried that you might have changed your mind" Joe finally said.

"I agreed, didn't I?" I stated with some annoyance.

"We just wanted to make sure. Nothing must go wrong".

"I know, I know, for Pete's sake. I gave you my word, didn't I?

"Just making sure" said Joe.

I could tell from the brevity of his conversation that he was uncomfortable questioning me, and I guessed that he was being forced by his accomplices to be sure that I carried out my side of the deal that had been made weeks ago.

"Joe" I said with a reassuring tone "I'll do as we planned, I'll lie low, I'll be inconspicuous, and no one will suspect anything. I won't spend a dime. In fact I'm thinking of being a good husband and father for a change and asking the family if they would like to spend a vacation in some out of the way place, where no one will recognize me or even give a damn as to who I am"

"Now you're thinking along the right track" Joe replied, the relief evident in his voice "go and enjoy yourself, the sooner the better, and stay as long as you want, in fact the longer the better".

"Good bye Joe" I butted in "and don't worry, I'll call you in a few weeks when I get back"

I hung up the phone and considered the merits of my spontaneous suggestion. A family vacation might be both timely and fun, but where would we go?

I switched on the television; sometimes they advertised attractive vacation spots, maybe I'd get some ideas, I thought. I clicked my way from channel to channel until I finally found the Travel channel.

I watched for a while hoping for inspiration. I wasn't into skiing or hang gliding and I didn't enjoy sightseeing, museums, art galleries, historic places of interest, tourist traps or places with lots of people. The TV program was showing a long expanse of white sandy beach with beautiful turquoise water. I turned up the volume to find out where this idyllic place was located. The ad was for the Bahamas Out Islands, the Family Islands as they were called, what could be more perfect. The decision was practically made. Now all I had to do was convince the family that we were going on an extended vacation.

The news was not received well, in fact Annie, my 18 year old daughter made it very clear that there was absolutely no way that she would even consider a 'family' vacation to some remote deserted island.

"It's not a deserted island" I interjected in an effort to placate her, "in fact, I'm not exactly sure where I was planning to take you all, just one of these Family Islands, it sounded ideal to me"

"You can go, and take Mum, but I'm not going!" she stated emphatically "what could I possibly do there with no friends and no movies. Hang out with a bunch of ignorant natives? You can't be serious?"

Annie was an only child, Daddy's little girl, who was no longer little or Daddy's anymore. She was smart, pretty as any movie actress, very mature for her almost eighteen years, very independent and spoiled. But to be fair she could have been a major problem, when in reality she was a wonderful girl and I was very proud of her. She had resisted most of the temptations that were constantly being faced by the young people of her generation. I had often thought of how I would have coped had I been a teenager of her generation, and I had concluded that I would probably have been one of worst kids on the block, into all the new fads, rings in my nose and other not so obvious places, purple hair, and a needle in my pocket.

"Let's talk to Mum when she gets home, see what she thinks" I pleaded.

"Dad, I'm not going. I don't care what Mum says."

Mum, my wife Laura, worked at the local library when she wasn't organizing a fund raiser for an environmental cause, of taking care of some less fortunate individual. We'd been married for nineteen years, and on a scale of one to ten, I would say our marriage was rated about a six. It had been as low as a two, but I'd worked hard to bring the rating up to an almost acceptable level, yet still it was far from perfect. Most of the problems had been of my making, and almost all the problems stemmed from the nature of my occupation. To put it bluntly I was a professional thief, a safe cracker. A much sought after expert in my field. I made a good living, provided for my family, was a good father and even though I say so myself, in all other aspects I was an excellent husband. I had learned to turn a deaf ear to the constant pleadings of Laura 'to get a real job'. I had a real job. I worked on both sides of the law, often helping the police in a robbery investigation, providing an exclusive service to several security firms and performing as an upstanding citizen of the community. Once in a while I strayed off the straight and narrow and supplemented my income by helping some other less fortunate thieves in their chosen profession. Was that so terrible? Laura thought it was.

Annie got her good looks from Laura, I take no credit for her beauty, but I do take credit for her smartness and independence. Laura is a 'good' person. I'm not. Many of my friends think I'm good, but not in the same context as Laura, there are different levels of goodness. I'm good at what I do, I'm a good provider, a good parent, a good listener but I'm a scoundrel. An opportunist is the way I would choose to describe myself. I just can't turn the other cheek when I see an opportunity to make a few extra quid. Whereas Laura doesn't have a dishonest bone in her body, she's reliable, caring, genuinely interested in people's problems and always available to provide a helping hand.

Twenty years ago when we first met, Laura was overwhelmed with adoration for me. She had never met anyone like me, not surprising really when you consider that I am rather unique. I literally swept her off her feet She feel deeply in love with me, and even to this day, in spite of all my short comings I know that she still loves me. I know that I'm a lucky man. Annie had added a new dimension to our lives, I had even given serious consideration to going 'straight', but I didn't, I just became better at my job and more careful.

I heard Laura's car drive up to the garage and momentarily she burst into the kitchen with her arms loaded with bags of groceries, books and a variety of other things.

"I'm home" she called.

I jumped up to meet her and take the bags from her grasp, "how was your day?" I inquired.

"Oh, the usual, busy, busy. Where's Annie?"

"On the phone" I replied. I had no idea where she was, but 'on the phone' was most likely where she was.

I kissed her on the lips as I helped her with the bags, she looked at me with a question in her eyes "Wow, what did I do to deserve that?"

"Is there something wrong about kissing my wife" I asked jokingly.

"No, of course not, you took me by surprise" She took off her coat and kicked her shoes off, "that's better, now lets try that again".

She fitted herself into my arms and turned her face to mine as we kissed long and passionately.

"Welcome home" I murmured.

"That's quite the welcome" she purred, "I think I'll go out and come back in again".

Laura was wearing a dark blue skirt and a simple white blouse, that on most women would have looked just plain ordinary, but on Laura it looked like a high fashion models selection. She had a natural beauty about her and a figure that made all her clothes look just right. Her hair was disheveled, and her make up had disappeared during the course of the day, but she was still ravishing. She smiled as she sat down with a sigh on one of the kitchen chairs, "Annie" she shouted, "I'm home".

"I'm on the phone" Annie called, "I'll be right there"

I smiled to myself knowing that I had guessed correctly. Annie spent hours on the telephone talking to her girl friends in hushed tones. Her own telephone had been her only request for her sixteenth birthday, and as I had said to Laura, the cost of the phone was only the tip of the iceberg; it was the monthly bills that would be mounting up that would be a continuing cause of friction.

"I was thinking of taking you all out to dinner" I stated.

"That'll be nice" Laura answered "what's the occasion?"

"No special occasion, I want to ask you something, and over dinner seems the best way".

"Ah! You want something" she teased "I knew it".

Married people have a way of understanding many things about their chosen partners that are not exactly secret, but are not always obvious even to the particular partner. Laura had this sixth sense, an uncanny way of knowing me better than I knew myself. Very often it was a shrug of my shoulders, a slight change in the pitch of my voice or some other give away sign that alerted her to a problem, or a request or even to a situation that I was hardly aware of myself. She knew the signs.

"You're planning another job?" she said accusingly.

"No!" I replied "I'm not, I promise"

"It's something you know I won't like?"

"Not at all" I said "it's a surprise that's all. I'll tell you over dinner"

"Have you told Annie?" Laura asked.

"About dinner? No."

"Where are you taking us?"

"I thought we'd go to Maxime's. Live it up a little".

"Really, you know I love it there. This must be a big surprise" she laughed.

She got up from the kitchen table, reached up and kissed me.

"I'll go and get ready, put on my party shoes".

7

Laura hummed as she went upstairs. "We're going out to dinner Annie" she called, "hurry up and get changed, we don't want to keep our date waiting".

While the 'girls' were preening I decided to make a reservation. Although it was a weekday Maxime's was a popular spot and often had a line of people waiting for tables. The owner was a sorta friend of mine, if you get my meaning, and a quick call was all it took to get the best table in the house.

Annie came down from upstairs first, she hadn't changed and from the look on her face it was evident that she had no intention of accompanying us to dinner.

"Annie! Sweetheart! You're not coming?"

"No, you two go. Have a good time, see if you can sell Mum on your crazy idea" she said.

"I wish I could change your mind, about both".

"Not a chance" Annie replied as she picked her phone and dialed one of her friends.

"Did you mention anything to your Mother about the trip" I asked.

"Not a word." she answered.

I made myself a drink while I waited for Laura. "Can I bring you up a drink?" I called.

"No thanks, I'll wait until we're there".

By now Annie was in an intense conversation with one of her buddies and had tuned out the real world. I could barely hear her voice, she seemed to be listening more than talking. That's good I thought, takes after her old man. I took my drink into the living room and switched on the TV. It was still tuned into the Travel channel, and the same ad was running for the Family Islands of the Bahamas. It must be a sign I surmised, we are meant to visit them. As I watched, the program displayed more pictures of fish, coral reefs, divers, quaint little houses and narrow quiet roads. The screen scrolled down a list of names, The Exumas, Harbour Island, Long Island, Spanish Wells, Eleuthera and Cat Island, it all looked exotic to me. I was so engrossed in the program that I didn't hear Laura enter the room.

"What are you watching?" she asked.

"Oh! Nothing, just what was on, some sorta travelogue. You look very sexy in that dress; you'll be the prettiest girl in the restaurant. You know Annie's not coming with us?"

"Yes, she's got a project to finish by tomorrow".

Maxime's was busy. A line of people were waiting for tables and the bar was overflowing with patrons who had reservations but who's tables were not ready or were still occupied. I saw Laura's expression change as she anticipated a long wait and with the wait a change in her mood.

"Let's go some place else" she said.

"Just be patient" I told her.

I caught the eye of the overwhelmed hostess, she smiled and beckoned me over. "Mr. Perinni is waiting for" she said.

She motioned us to follow her as she led the way to the best table in the house. I slipped her a tenner and thanked her. Al Perinni vacated his chair and held it out for Laura to take "Have a nice evening folks" he said as patted my shoulder and excused himself.

"Who was that?" asked Laura.

"Just a friend of mine, he owns the place" I replied, trying to act like it was no big deal.

"Well, I must say that you sure know how to impress a girl. This could turn out to be an interesting date. Do you come here often?" she hesitated, "don't answer that. I don't want to know".

"I did a job for him a while ago. He said he owed me, so I called to make a reservation just in case this place was busy, I'm glad I did".

"I feel kinda special, I'm sure everyone is wondering who we are".

"Most likely trying to figure out what a great looking girl like you is doing with a creep like me" I retorted.

"You're probably right" Laura agreed.

"Thanks" I said humbly, "You sure know how to build up a nervous guy's confidence".

"You, nervous! That'll be the day".

The waiter came over to take our drinks order. We decided on a 1972 Bordeaux, and asked him to bring the wine before our food, we both enjoy sipping wine, and I had found through experience that good wine had a great soothing effect on us both. We looked through the menu and decided to have the Rack of Lamb for Two, one of the specialties of the house.

The waiter returned with the wine and poured a little in my glass for me to taste, which I did and nodded my approval, "Very nice" I mumbled.

"Thank you, sir, it's with the compliments of Mr. Perinni" said the waiter.

"What exactly did you do for this character" asked Laura suspiciously.

"Nothing much" I answered, "just knocked off his wife for him" I joked.

Laura laughed and relaxed. She was enjoying my company, the free wine, and the special treatment. Now I thought is a good time to broach the subject of the trip.

"Honey, how does a trip to the Bahamas sound?"

"Sounds wonderful" she replied, "why, do you know someone who's going?"

"I meant for us, just the two of us. Annie doesn't want to go".

"You talked to Annie about it?"

"This afternoon"

"What's the occasion? What brought this on?"

"I have to leave town, disappear for a while, and lie low"

"When are you planning to go?"

"Tomorrow or the next day, sooner the better was the exact advice that I was given."

"I can't possibly get away on such short notice. I have a million things to do and I'm committed for most of next week. There's no way I can go, and I don't like to be told to leave town".

"I'm sorry" I muttered, "I was really hoping we could enjoy a vacation together. Maybe you could come later" I suggested.

"That's a possibility, where are you planning to go?"

"To the Bahamas, one of the Family Islands, where it's quiet and secluded, off the beaten track. Where no one will recognize me".

"Sounds wonderful".

11

We talked about the various places that I had seen in the ad on the TV; Laura was enthralled with the sound of Spanish Wells and picked it as her first choice.

"Maybe you can get to practice your Spanish there" she commented.

"Or fall down one of the wells" I added.

We both welcomed the silence as we ate our lamb, I knew only too well that she was upset about my need to 'get lost', and it added yet more ammunition to her reasons for me to be completely rid of my associations with people like Al Perinni. I was not looking forward to our ride home together, knowing that I would be in for another lecture and a possible ultimatum regarding our future. I could almost see the words 'get a real job' on her lips. We managed to enjoy the rest of the evening, including the after dinner drinks courtesy of Mr. Perinni, and when we finally made ready to leave he was right at hand to make sure that I 'kept in touch' with him and that 'we were welcome anytime'. Laura was polite and thanked him for all his trouble; I shook his hand and said I'd stay in contact.

Laura was quiet during the drive home. Only when we were undressed and in bed with the light off did she say anything, and then she voiced her feelings with so much anger that it made me wish that I hadn't asked her to accompany me.

'Don't call me when you're away" she said coldly "I don't want to hear about the good time you're having, or the great people you've met".

I was on the verge of telling her that she was being unreasonable, but decided that there was no point. Her mind was made up and the subject was closed. I would be going to Spanish Wells alone.

CHAPTER TWO

After consulting with a travel agent, I decided to fly into Nassau, stay over and then continue on to Spanish Wells by Ferry boat the next morning. The other alternative would have been to fly to Miami and then on to North Eleuthera. My departure was a sad affair, although no tears were shed, my wife and daughter had obviously made a secret alliance to show no emotion and to only wish me good luck.

"We'll see you when you get back" they both said as if they had rehearsed the same lines.

After a dutiful hug from Annie and a peck on the cheek from Laura, I climbed into my waiting taxi and headed for the airport.

Going away on my own was not a daunting experience for me, I really enjoyed it. For most of my life I had been a loner, the very nature of my work made me a cautious person and friendships were always guarded and difficult to maintain. Even though I had had visions of Laura, Annie and me having a normal family vacation, I was not too disappointed with their decision not to join me. I could do my own thing, whatever that was, and some of those obligatory family excursions were not much enjoyment for me. So with my head held high, plenty of cash in my pocket, a wardrobe of casual clothes packed into my suitcases, I made my way to the check- in line at the airport.

The weather at the time of my departure was unpleasant, with drizzling rain and a cold wind; I looked forward to arriving in Nassau where I expected the sun to be shining and the temperature to be at least eighty degrees. The British Airways flight was almost full, with a lot of excited kids going on their first tropical holiday, many Bahamians returning home after visiting relatives in England and thanking God that they didn't live there, plus a few odd balls, like me I suppose, whose mission or purpose could not be determined. My traveling companion was a girl of about the same age as Annie, I guessed that she was Bahamian, but she could have been from just about anywhere in the Caribbean. Fortunately there was a vacant seat between us which allowed us to spread out and find some additional room for the collection of goodies that the flight attendants continually thrust upon us, but never seemed to be ready to retrieve.

"Are you going home?" I asked.

"Yes" my companion replied, "I attend University here".

"What are you studying?" I inquired in an attempt to make her less apprehensive.

"Criminology" she said proudly "I'm a lawyer"

"Oh! Shit" I muttered, "just my luck!"

"Excuse me" she said.

"Nothing, I was talking to myself. You hardly look old enough to be a lawyer".

"Oh, I'm old enough. Are you staying in Nassau?"

"I'm only staying overnight. I'm on my way to Spanish Wells".

She actually laughed and put her hand to her mouth to cover her embarrassment, "You must be kiddin'" she said.

"No I'm serious; I'm going to Spanish Wells. Why is that so funny to you?"

"I'm sorry" she said "not many tourists travel there, it's different".

"I'm not your regular tourist type" I responded defensively "I happen to enjoy places that are different".

"Then you'll really like Spanish Wells".

Lunch was being served so our conversation came to an end. Her reaction to my intended destination bothered me. Why did she laugh when I mentioned Spanish Wells? Surely some people went there for vacations, the few pictures I'd seen were beautiful and featured long sandy beaches, quaint houses and streets, and a colorful collection of fishing boats. It all looked pretty normal to me.

My travel plans were skimpy to say the least, I was to arrive in Nassau, then take a taxi to the British Colonial Hotel. Tomorrow I was scheduled to board the Bahamas Fast Ferry for the trip to Spanish Wells, where I was booked into the Adventurers Hotel for an undetermined length of time. How long was I planning to stay? What was I expecting to accomplish? I really hadn't given the subject much thought, play it by ear was the plan, and be ready for anything, and above all stay inconspicuous.

"Is this your fist time in the Bahamas?" my traveling companion asked.

"Yes. How did you guess?"

"I saw you looking at the change the air hostess gave to you; I could tell that you were unfamiliar with our colorful bills".

"Observed like a true attorney" I joked "by the way I'm David".

I extended my hand across the spare seat between us; she grasped my hand and shook it with a firm almost masculine grip.

"Nice to meet you, my name's Melanie Pinder"

"Were you born in Nassau?"

"No" Melanie replied "I'm from Harbour Island, I'm a Brillander".

"I have no idea where that is"

"It's just a few miles from Spanish Wells actually, but is totally different. Harbour Island was once the capital of the Bahamas. It's old and very picturesque, with one of the best beaches in the world. You must make sure that you visit for a few days, it would be a shame to be so close and not see it all".

"If it's so beautiful, why did you leave?"

"I went to school in Nassau, and then to University in England. The schools here are not particularly good if you want to further your education".

"Do you plan to fly to Harbour Island?" I inquired.

"No, I'll take the BoHengy tomorrow"

"The what?" I laughed.

"The ferry, it's called the BoHengy. I know there's a story behind the name but for the life of me I can't recall what it is".

"Is this the Fast Ferry? The same one that will get me to Spanish Wells?"

17

"Yes, the boat stops in Spanish Wells then continues on to Harbour Island, it's about a half hour ride further on".

At any other time I would have seized this opportunity to get to know this attractive young lady. She was pretty, and obviously very intelligent with a wonderful openness about her. While we had been talking I had noticed that she looked directly into my eyes and seemed to smile all the time. Her teeth glistened like those you see in toothpaste commercials. My first reaction had been that she was barely older than my daughter, but now I was estimating that she was closer to twenty five or maybe twenty eight. She had a youthfulness about her that defied an accurate guess as to her age. It was hard to imagine her as a lawyer. I thought of the many times I had had legal counsel none of my representatives had looked at all like her. Pretty girls have an unfair advantage in every walk of life, and an attorney that looked like Melanie would capture the sympathy of any judge that I had ever encountered. I reminded myself to make sure I collected one of her business cards; you never know when you might need a lawyer, especially in my line of work.

"Penny for your thoughts" she interrupted.

"I was miles away" I answered, "Thinking about you actually. Do you have a business card?"

She fumbled through her purse and handed me her card. I slipped it into my pocket.

"You never know, I might need a good lawyer one day" I said, "especially one as pretty as you".

If her skin had been a different color, I believe I would have seen her blush.

The seat belt sign came on, and I could feel the plane start to descend. I looked out of the window as we approached Nassau and watched the miles of turquoise water, the golden beaches and hotels, pass below us.

"We're here" she said.

"I'll look for you tomorrow, on the BoHengy" I laughed.

After we deplaned, Melanie disappeared into the terminal and was cleared through customs quickly as a returning resident. I waited in line, for my turn to be interrogated by immigration. A group of musicians were playing a selection of old Harry Belafonte tunes, I recognized 'This is my Island in the Sun', and thought that this vacation was going to be exactly what the doctor had ordered. Immigration and customs were an easy formality, I passed through without any problems and was soon outside in the warm sunshine, it felt so good. A taxi appeared from out of no where, and soon I was on my way to the British Colonial.

The hotel was located downtown and within walking distance of banks, churches, stores and cafes. My room was nicely furnished and looked to be quite new, there was no mini bar, but there were two large beds, a very well appointed bathroom with a stack of fluffy towels piled on the vanity and a balcony overlooking the pool area.

I decide to go for a walk to get a flavour of the Bahamas and to have my first encounter with the natives. Maybe I'd sample some of the local food. The straw market was located adjacent to the hotel, but there was nothing there that caught my eye. I did however, find that the majority of the merchandise was made in places other than the Bahamas. The local women were colourful and loud, and seemed to be doing well by taking advantage of the hundreds of tourists that had arrived earlier in the day aboard several large cruise ships.

I sauntered along Bay Street enjoying the warm temperature, and observing the unusual custom of the traffic driving on the left, just like England, but with most of the cars having the driver on the left hand side. It seemed like a disaster waiting to happen.

My desire for a sampling of the local cuisine was soon relegated to having to endure the same fast food establishments as every other city in the world. MacDonald's, Burger King and Kentucky Fried Chicken dominated every corner. I turned into a side street to find a more secluded restaurant where I could have a drink and dinner. I lost track of the turns I had made and the number of cross streets I had passed. A small sign above a darkened door caught my attention, I pushed my way in and found what appeared to be an English pub. I ordered a pint of Courage Ale and settled into a seat at the bar. Just like home. The patrons were friendly, polite and curious about my stay in Nassau and particularly about my intended visit to Spanish Wells. In fact the mere mention of Spanish Wells brought a mixture of odd reactions from all those within hearing distance of me.

"Will someone please tell me what the problem with Spanish Wells is?" I asked, "every time I mention the place, I receive strange knowing looks, smiles or outright laughter from just about everybody".

"It's different" somebody replied.

"Weird" another voice injected.

"A man sent a package to Spanish Wells on the mail boat, and three times it came back", one of the patrons of the bar relayed this story, "finally the boss inquired as to what the problem was, the man on the boat said that when he went to deliver the package in Spanish Wells the fella on the dock said that he'd lived there all his life, and that there weren't anybody by the name of Fragile livin' there!"

This brought a burst of enthusiastic laughter from all within hearing distance, even though I was fairly certain that most of them had the story more than once before.

"Did you hear about the fella from Spanish Wells that was in Florida and he locked his keys in his car", somebody else chimed in. "he called the police on his cell phone and they said it would be a while before they could get to him. He answered that they'd better hurry 'cause his wife and kids were also locked inside"

The jokes came one after the other, it became obvious to me that the people of Spanish Wells were the brunt of the local jokesters much like the jokes directed in fun at the Polish and the Newfies.

"Enough" I laughed, "I get it now, but why".

An older man, who had never said a word during all the fun that I had unintentionally been at the center of, leaned over to me and said in a quiet voice "They're interbred with one another. Uncles, cousins, brothers and sisters, they're strange, half of them are a bit simple and the other half are locked up in their attics, out of sight and out of the way."

"He's right" the man on the adjacent bar stool said, "they're all related in some way, there's only 1500 people there, and at least 500 of them are named Pinder!"

"I met a girl on the plane whose name was Pinder, she said she was from Harbour Island",

"Could well be" replied my neighbor, "they're spread out pretty good all across the Bahamas, you'll find Pinders of both colours, but not in Spanish Wells".

"D'you mean that there are no people of colour there?"

"You don't have to polite about it" someone said "tell it like it is, there aint no black people there. At least what lives there. Just a couple of Government employees like a policeman and a customs guy, and maybe a couple of school teachers, but everybody else is white".

"I had no idea" I said, "never gave it a thought actually. Just one policeman eh!"

"And he has nothing to do. Best job on the force if you can stand bein' in Spanish Wells all yer life!"

"So there's very little crime?" I asked.

"None at all" one of the patrons responded, "that is if you don't count drug smugglin'".

Everyone nodded in agreement.

"Yes sir. There's some mighty rich people there, what's made a fortune from drugs".

"I'll drink to that!"

"Course they're all Christians" someone said sarcastically.

The conversation continued through the evening, and I got a real insight into the peculiarities and traditions of the people of Spanish Wells, at least from the biased perspective of the patrons of The Green Shutters. I decided to stay and have dinner, rather than seek out another restaurant. Eddie, one of the bar crowd said he'd join me, so we moved into the adjacent dining room to order dinner.

The menu featured English pub food. I settled on steak and kidney pie. So much for my venture into sampling the local cuisine.

"Why are you going to Spanish Wells?" Eddie asked.

"No reason, I just it picked because of the name".

"Are you going up on the Bohengy?"

"Yes, in the morning" I answered.

"You'll enjoy the ride. The weather will be fine, no storms in the forecast".

"How long is the trip?"

"I believe it's about an hour and twenty minutes. You leave Potters Cay at eight and arrive in Spanish Wells at nine thirty. Then the boat continues on to Dunmore Town".

I assumed that Dunmore Town was on Harbour Island, as this confirmed the information given to me on the plane by Melanie.

"I'm going there to relax and do nothing" I commented.

"That's good, 'cause there's nothing to do there anyway".

"From the pictures I've seen, it looks very quaint".

"It is. The people work hard, and they enjoy a better life style than any other Bahamians, almost everyone fishes for a living, mostly for crawfish".

"That's lobster?" I commented.

"Yes, Spiny Lobster, unlike Maine lobster, it has no claws, all the meat is in the tail. And it's delicious, make sure you try some". Eddie continued.

"So, if I understand you all correctly, these weird people in Spanish Wells are hard working Christians, who make a bundle of money catching lobsters, and they spend their hard earned money raising their families in a crime free environment. And they're all white!" I stated emphatically.

"That's about it".

"I think there's a little jealousy involved here. Isn't there?"

"Maybe" Eddie conceded.

I looked at the time and realized that I'd been up for almost twenty hours. I insisted on paying for dinner, and then said my goodbyes to Eddie and the other patrons still sitting at the bar. To a chorus of 'have a good trip', 'come back anytime', 'don't get in any trouble', and a mixture of farewells, I finally made it to the door and out into the street. It was still very warm. I followed the directions I had been given and soon I was back on Bay Street, I turned left and could now see the Hotel a few blocks away. I enjoyed the short walk and a few minutes later I turned into the Western entrance of the hotel. I asked the friendly girl at the desk if she could arrange for a taxi to Potters Cay for first thing in the morning. She suggested that I should be ready to leave at 7 o'clock.

Potters Cay is a local market place, where you can buy fresh fish, fresh conch, fruit and vegetables and other locally grown or locally caught delicacies. It is situated beneath the bridge that connects New Providence to Paradise Island. The loading area for the BoHengy was at the end of the Cay, and it was here that the taxi dropped me.

"The ticket office is right there" the driver said, as he pointed towards a construction trailer that was being used as an office.

I bought a round trip ticket, even though I had no idea when I might be returning. The ferry boat was a thing of beauty. It looked new. The exterior was painted to look like an underwater scene, with reef fish, and coral heads, all on a blue background. The interior was like a 747 with plenty of comfortable seats for everyone. I chose to sit outside, and I made my way up to the open upper deck. The big diesels were started and soon we were underway. One of the crew explained that we would be traveling 'on the inside' because of the brisk wind that was blowing from the north west, this would mean that we would be staying close to land and at least I would have something to see. We exited Potters Cay and turned Eastwards with Paradise Island to our left. It reminded me of Monte Carlo, with fancy condos, hotels, expensive water front homes and even a championship golf course. Once we were passed the end of Paradise Island, the catamaran hulled ferry picked up speed as we proceeded on our way to Spanish Wells. I had a quick look around in the main cabin, but didn't see Melanie. I guessed that she was taking a later boat.

The journey was comfortable and uneventful. We passed many small islands, cays and rocks, but saw no signs of towns or people. The water was as blue as the sky and the boat captain maneuvered the vessel through some tight turns as he sought the deep channels between the submerged rocks, and coral heads. The passengers were a mixture of tourists, a group of school children on an outing, and residents of Spanish Wells and Harbour Island returning home from shopping trips or doctor's visits in Nassau. There was a buzz of excitement in the air, as I realized that for several of the passengers this was the first time they had taken the trip aboard this ferry. There was a constant flow of people visiting the refreshment counter, each person seeking some snack or other, to fortify them for having missed breakfast. I carried a sandwich up to the outside deck to enjoy the ride.

It was interesting to observe the unspoiled beauty of the area, and to realize how extensive the waters of the Bahamas were. It wasn't hard to understand that the majority of the inhabitants derived a living from the sea and that the fish population must be almost without end. The water was shallow as far as I could see, and it was so clear that I could see the bottom easily as we passed over grassy beds and coral out croppings. One of the crew announced that we were passing Pimlico Cay, and that Spanish Wells was just a few miles further ahead. I could see an island off to the port side with several nice modern homes, and as the boat slowed down, we entered the channel that led to the Government dock in Spanish Wells. As the boat slowly made its way through the narrow channel I had my first glimpse of my destination and the town that I had chosen to escape to. There was a sign over a brightly painted store that read 'Pinders Supermarket', another sign read 'Pinders Golf cart Rental' and yet another that read 'Pinders Boats'. I'm here, I said to myself, in Pinderland!

I was standing in line waiting to exit from the boat, when I felt a tug on my sleeve. It was Melanie.

"I thought I'd missed you" I said with surprise, "look at you, no wonder I didn't recognize you".

The gray business suit that she had worn on the plane had been replaced by a highly coloured off- the shoulder blouse and a pair of denim shorts. Her hair was down, and she wore a Yankees baseball cap on her head. She looked very different, yet still very desirable.

"You must have been up top" she stated.

"I was" I replied "doing the tourist thing".

"Enjoy your visit, and be sure to come to Dunmore Town".

"We'll have lunch" I proposed.

"I'd love to" she replied enthusiastically, "my number is 635".

It wasn't till much later that I discovered that all the numbers in Dunmore Town had the same first four digits, 333-2, so when people gave their phone numbers it was common for them to just provide the last three digits. Similarly in Spanish Wells all the phone numbers started with 333-4.

The passengers were now disembarking and I said a hurried farewell to Melanie.

"Call me" she mouthed.

"You can count on it" I answered as I waved goodbye.

I followed the other passengers down a short ramp and stepped onto the dock of Spanish Wells. I felt a little self conscious as I found myself scrutinizing the local people to see if they did look simple or malformed. But they all looked normal to me. I looked for a taxi to take me to the Adventures Hotel; my lost appearance must have been noticeable because a nice helpful lady, who I later learned was Linda Pinder, asked if she could help me.

"I need to get to the Adventures" I said.

"Best way is to rent a buggy" she suggested, "they have them right there".

I realized that a buggy was a golf cart, and it was the favorite mode of transport on the Island. Pinders Rentals was right at hand, so I rented a buggy for the month.

I headed west along a road which bordered the waterfront. There were boats of all sizes and descriptions tied up to the sea wall along the roadside, it was very obvious that this was a fishing town, and that everyone in town had at least one boat. The distance to the hotel was less than a mile, but even in this short distance I encountered more than a dozen cars, trucks or buggies and every one of the drivers waved to me as if I was an old friend. I waved back each time, and thought to myself that this would never happen in any other place in the world, where everybody is either suspicious of everyone else, or too busy to take the time to be friendly.

The Adventures Hotel was bigger and better than I had expected, the rooms were adequately furnished, and at the suggestion of the cute young lady in the office, who I later discovered was not a Pinder, I took a room that included a kitchen.

I hung my few good clothes in the closet, threw the rest of my things into one of the drawers of the bedroom dresser. I found just one bible, on the bedside night table, it seemed to be well used and there was a bookmark located on the page of the twenty third Psalm. I didn't have a problem with that. I took a quick shower and donned my casual clothes and immediately felt better.

By now it was only eleven o'clock and already it was very warm as I set off to explore the Island. My map showed that one road circumnavigated the entire island, while several others crossed the island from north to south. It was hard to get lost. The buggy had a top speed of about 10 miles per hour; in fact a couple of cyclists overtook me without breaking a sweat. All the houses were painted in a variety of bright colours, some green, some blue, even a few purple and pink. Their gardens were generally neat and well kept, with a wonderful variety of tropical plants and shrubs. Almost every house had a selection of chairs on their front porches, it was probably the coolest place to sit on a summers evening. I noticed that most of the other drivers were female, most were blond, blue eyed and pretty. They all waved as we passed. As the road meandered westwards I saw more large houses, more boats, and at the end of the island a bridge connecting Spanish Wells to another island, which I later learned was called Russell Island. I continued on past the bridge, turned north for a short distance and then east. A couple of small islands were located about a mile offshore, and the water between the beach and the islands looked as blue as any water I had ever seen. The temptation was too great. I pulled off to the side of the road, and jumped down onto the beach. There was no one around, so I shucked off my clothes and went for a swim. The water was warm but shallow, barely deep enough to swim and certainly too shallow to stand. I swam further out and the water depth slowly increased. Just what the doctor ordered I thought. I closed my eyes and let the water wash over me.

"Hey" someone shouted.

I looked back towards the beach, wondering what the problem might be, a little annoyed at having my moment of meditation so rudely interrupted. There was a girl on the beach waving at me. Even from a distance I could see that she was attractive and was wearing a brief bathing suit. What she didn't now was that my swimming attire was considerably briefer than hers. I paddled on my hands and knees until I was within shouting range.

"What's the problem?" I inquired.

"You left the brake off on the buggy and it's rolled into the water" she called.

"Thanks" I said "I'll be right there, if you'll turn your back".

"You're naked?" she screamed. "Oh my God".

She turned away as I came into shallow water. I went to the buggy, retrieved my shorts, and went to introduce myself.

"Sorry about that" I said "I'm David".

She looked at me, keeping her eyes at head level.

"It's OK" she said, "I'm Chris".

"Nice to meet you" I said, "are you from here?"

"Yes" she answered "I was born here. Where are you from?"

"England. Just arrived this morning, it's a bit warmer than where I came from".

"You don't see many local people on the beach" she continued "but I love the beach and like to walk here every day".

"Then I'll see you again. I'm a beach person too".

"Bye" she smiled and she continued on her way along the beach.

If Chris was a sample of the local population, then those crazy people in The Green Shutters must be totally mistaken. Not only was she pretty, friendly and obviously happy, but she was considerably better than normal. I felt quite elated with the encounter, and was looking forward to meeting Chris again. So far so good and I'd only been here for a few hours.

My next mission was lunch. I had noticed two restaurants on the Island, and I knew that if I continued driving east, I would eventually make a full circle and pass the restaurants once again. I was now on the road that paralleled the beach side of Spanish Wells, here the beach front lots were secluded and I could see several large imposing homes. There must be of great deal of money around here, I speculated, I wonder if it all comes from crawfish or other legal means?

I was now reentering the town from the west; I passed a large supermarket, a gym and game room, a bakery, a couple of service stations, a nursery and another restaurant named the Gap. I parked the buggy, sniffed the appetizing aromas emanating from within, and entered.

Another blond goddess handed me a menu as I sat down. She asked me how I was doin', then recited the specials of the day. I settled on stewed Turbot, one of the patrons of the Green Shutters had mentioned to me that I should not miss this authentic Bahamian dish.

The food was excellent, but the portion was sufficient for at least two people. The waitress was kind enough to provide a takeout box for the leftovers, so I paid my bill and headed back to the hotel for a snooze.

My room was freezing cold from the very efficient air conditioning; I adjusted the temperature and decided a snooze on the beach was a better plan. This time I wore my swim suit. I carried a towel and a copy of Nelson Demille's newest book with me, as I headed for a relaxing afternoon on the beach. I felt like hanging a sign around my neck that read 'I'm on vacation, do not bother me'. If only Laura and Annie could see me now, I doubt that they had ever seen me in such a contented state. This was the life!

The beach on the North side of the Island was fabulous, more than a mile of soft golden sand. There were no people, no one selling anything, no food vendors, no noisy ski doos, just a tranquility that has become a rarity in today's bustling society. The water was shallow for several hundred yards offshore, perfect for kids and non swimmers, and after a short nap in the hot sun, I was more than ready to lie in the shallow water and let the world pass me by.

CHAPTER THREE

I parked my buggy outside Pinders Supermarket, while I shopped for a few basic necessities that I found that I needed, in the morning it was more convenient to make a cup of tea or to have an apple or a grapefruit for breakfast, than having to get dressed and drive to one of the three restaurants.

As I emerged from the store I noticed that two fishing boats had arrived during the night or the early hours of the morning. They were tied up at the end of the Government dock amidst a throng of cars and trucks, there seemed to be a lot of activity taking place, and not wanting to miss out on anything of interest, I drove down to take a look.

The boats were unloading crawfish. Bags and bags of crawfish, frozen solid and packed in forty pound bags. The bags were being off loaded into a stainless steel box that was then being moved by a fork lift to a cold storage freezer at the local sea food wholesalers. This process had been going on for some time before I had arrived, and evidently would continue on for several more hours after I had left.

The crew from the boat was watching patiently from the deck as each bag was counted and given a cursory check. This was an important day for them, the culmination of a three week fishing trip and more importantly, this was pay day.

When the final bag had been unloaded, the wholesaler conferred with the spokesman for the crew, I assumed that this was the captain; their totals were checked and rechecked, and final number was agreed upon. The wholesaler counted out a stack of hundred dollar bills and passed them to the captain, who in turn paid each man according to his share.

I sat and watched with a look of incredulity on my face. Had I really seen what I knew that I had seen? Had this whole transaction taken place with cash? There must have been thousands of dollars that changed hands, and this was just one out of the total of thirty boats in the fishing fleet. Oh my goodness, I thought, what have I unknowingly stumbled onto?

I waited and watched as the second boat was unloaded. The final result was exactly the same. It was beyond belief!

"That's a lotta crawfish"

I looked around to see if the remark had been directed towards me. It was the local cop, watching the proceedings from his buggy.

"I've never seen so much" I responded.

"This is a record year" he added "bin catchin' more an' more each season".

Before I could ask him how much they expected to catch this season, he volunteered "Wouldn't be surprised if they passed the two million pound mark".

"Really, that much?" I said.

He answered my next question before I could ask it "At ten to twelve dollars a pound, that's a lotta money!"

"You're right" I commented "It's a fortune".

I tried to put the whole scene out of my mind; I was here to lie low, to be inconspicuous, not to try to figure out a way to rip off the local fishermen. But I had to admit to myself that the temptation was monumental. I knew that even without wanting to, I would put together the pieces of a scheme to steal the money without getting caught. The chances of ever putting such a scheme into action were slim, I knew that, but I just couldn't resist the challenge.

The evening before, I had called home to tell Laura how much I missed her, and to try once again to get her to join me. She was in high spirits, saying that she missed me too, and that she hoped I was staying out of trouble. She never asked me anything about Spanish Wells, or what I was doing every day, she rambled on about all the activities that she was involved with, explaining in no uncertain terms, that it was impossible for her to even think of taking a short weekend vacation.

At least I'd tried.

On one of my tours around the island I had encountered a fishing guide; he had talked to me about taking a trip with him out to the Dutch Bar. At first I thought this might be a place where you could buy Heineken beer, but he informed that the Dutch Bar was one of the best fishing grounds in the area. It was about 5 miles offshore to the Northwest of Spanish Wells, an area where there was a drop off, a sharp change in the configuration of the ocean bottom, a place where large fish came to find smaller prey. Our plan was to leave early the next morning at seven and to be back with our catch, by noon.

I had never enjoyed fishing, on the numerous trips that I had taken, I had never caught any fish of any size, the weather had never cooperated, and I usually came home looking like a drowned rat with nothing to show for the effort or the discomfort. I hoped that today it would be different.

I met Little Willy at the Yacht Haven marina. LW as I referred to him, had already caught a dozen pilchards that we would be using as bait to catch Tuna and Dolphin. He explained that Dolphin is a fish and not a relative of Flipper.

We traveled west by boat, under the bridge to Russell Island, then headed north past Pierre Rock and out into the ocean. The boat was 18 feet long with a one hundred and fifteen horse power engine. A bimini top protected us from the blazing sun, and LW had plenty of lines, gaffs and nets. He was well prepared to catch fish. The ocean was calm, and soon we were in the deep water where the fish were supposed to be. With the motor off it was very peaceful; LW baited two lines, tossed a few pilchards into the water, and waited. Within minutes my line went tight as a fish hit the bait, the nylon line streamed from the reel as the fish ran hard trying to escape. I stood up, placed the rod into my rod holder and began to reel in the line. A blue and yellow fish broke the surface about 50 feet away.

"It's a dolphin, about 20 lbs. A bull" yelled LW.

As the fish was pulled close to the boat, he reached over, grabbed the wire leader and hauled the fish into the boat. A quick rap on the head quieted the fish down and then LW put it into the fish well.

"That's a good start" I laughed excitedly, just as the other line tightened.

"There's another one. Haul her in"

We caught 5 fish in less than an hour. They all had the same beautiful colours, but the first one was the biggest. LW decided to move to another spot to try for tuna. He baited the hooks with live pilchards and let the bait sink to the bottom. After about 15 minutes my line took a hit, I grabbed the rod and jerked hard to set the hook and started to wind in the line. It felt like a ton of bricks on the end of the line and soon I was sweating with the effort. My arms were aching, my back was sore, and my legs were trembling as I continued to reel the line in inch by inch.

"Must be a huge fish" I commented.

"Tuna" he confirmed.

"It's so strong".

"Its way down, let's hope the sharks don't get it"

"Sharks?" I started to say. Just then the pressure on the line slackened and I reeled in the balance of the line only to discover that the sharks had got it. All that was left was the Tuna's head and about a quarter of the fish's upper body. The rest had been eaten in one giant bite, the teeth marks evident on the Tuna's skin.

"That fish must've weighed 50 or 60 pounds" I stated "The shark must have been a monster".

We caught 4 more Tuna, but never landed one. All we landed were the remains, after the sharks had had their share.

"Is it always like this? I asked.

"Usually, though it never used to be. The sharks know where we fish, and they wait below for us to do the work".

"Can you catch them?"

"We do. But we're not supposed to. Sharks are a protected species".

LW decided that we had had enough for one day; he wound in the lines, gunned the engine and headed home.

Back at the dock, I watched as he skillfully cleaned the Dolphin. They yielded more than 40 pounds of fillet, which he packaged neatly in zippered plastic bags.

Because I had paid for the trip, the fish was theoretically mine. I had no use for all the bags of fillet; I took one bag, plenty for a good meal, and told LW that he could have the balance.

"How shall I cook it?" I asked.

"Marinate it in sour or lime for an hour, then grill it. Or marinate it in Zesty Italian."

I wasn't sure what he meant by Zesty Italian, but I didn't want to ask and appear to be naïve, so I collected my things from the boat, picked up my bag of fish and headed back to the hotel.

It had been an unforgettable experience, the one fishing trip that I would remember for years to come. After I showered, I caught a glimpse of myself in the full length mirror on the back of the bathroom door; I struck a manly pose and was pleased to see how tanned and fit I looked.

Island life agreed with me. The absence of daily stress caused by busy schedules, traffic jams, and the necessary interaction between people, were all missing here. The knowledge that I had no plans and no time table had a soothing effect on me. I hadn't had a drink since I had arrived, not that I'm an alcoholic, but on a warm day, like today had been, a cold beer would have tasted wonderful. The thought of the beer lingered with me as I strolled down to the waterfront. I boarded the Government ferry to Jean's Bay, paid $4 for a round trip ticket, and in 10 minutes I was on the mainland of North Eleuthera where beer and liquor were readily available. I purchased a case of Kalik, the locally brewed beer, a couple of bottles of wine, a bottle of Anejo Rum and carried my elicit purchase back to the ferry.

I was expecting to hear about the evils of drinking from the ferry boat driver, but he laughed when he heard of my concern about bringing 'booze' into Spanish Wells. He told me, without me prompting him, that he would guess that more than half the population imbibed, and that the incidence of alcoholism was quite high on the island. This just reinforced my long held opinion, that if you ban any product from the market, people will find a way to purchase it and abuse it. It's human nature.

I decided to call Melanie. She answered on the second ring, recognized my voice immediately, called to someone to turn down the radio, and asked how I was doin'.

"I'm doin' fine" I teased. "I'm planning to come to Harbour Island tomorrow on the Bohengy, and I'm hoping that you'll let me buy you lunch?"

"Tomorrow's fine, I'd love it".

"Where shall we meet?"

"I'll meet you at the dock where the Bohengy ties up; this is your first time here, right?"

"You know it is".

"Then I'll give you the grand tour. Are you going back in the afternoon?"

"I was" I replied "But I can easily change my mind. I have no plans!"

"Bring your tooth brush; you never know what may happen".

"I'm ready for anything" I joked "I'm looking forward to seeing you".

"Me too" she said enthusiastically, "I'll see you tomorrow. Bye".

Was that an invitation? Now I was in a quandary. Should I pack an overnight bag, or should I resist the temptation, behave like a happily married man, have a nice lunch and return to my hotel for the night? I flipped a coin. I had to make it the best two out of three to get the result I wanted. I needed to carry a bag anyway, I rationalized, I would need a towel, and a swim suit, sure I could wear the swim suit under my shorts, but I'd never liked that, everything would remain wet and uncomfortable. And if I purchased a few gifts to take home, then I had a bag to carry them in. Having resolved yet another problem in my daily life, I found that I was uneasy with the feelings of anticipation I was having. Maybe she was just being friendly, it was her natural demeanor, I'm sure I was getting the wrong signals, hearing what I wanted to hear, and jumping to the wrong conclusion. Play it cool would be my game plan, and above all, don't make a fool of myself.

The Bohengy was on time the next morning. There were a lot of returning residents disembarking, most loaded down with bags and boxes filled with merchandise they had purchased in Nassau. I waited until they had all vacated the ferry, then I handed my ticket to the check-in person and boarded. I made my way to the top deck, found a seat on the starboard side, as the boat moved away from the dock.

The trip to Harbour Island takes about half an hour, and involves a passage inside of the Devil's Backbone, a treacherous coral reef that has claimed many shipwrecks over the years. Most private yachts that make this trip, hire a local pilot, however the captain of the Bohengy was adequately accomplished and knowledgeable, and able to make the passage every day without mishap. I watched carefully as the boat turned into the deep waters between the coral heads; at one point in the journey it was necessary for the boat to come very close to the beach to avoid hitting some submerged rocks. I had an appreciation of the skill of the captain and wondered how the boat would survive in a nasty storm or when the surf was running high. I later found out that they remained in Spanish Wells during a 'rage', the local name for bad sea conditions, and only made this trip when conditions were suitable.

After we were through the Devil's Backbone, the water calmed and soon we were approaching Dunmore Town. It was a pretty sight from a distance, with little houses of all colours and sizes perched on the hillsides that sloped gently to the blue waters of the sound.

Melanie waved to me as I descended onto the Dunmore Town dock. I made my way through the throngs of people, all of them hugging and kissing as if they had been parted for a decade, when most had only been away for a day or two.

She hugged me enthusiastically; it must be a Brilander tradition, I thought.

"Welcome to Harbour Island" she announced "my name is Melanie, and I'll be your tour guide for the day".

She handed me a plastic cup, then raised her own cup to me in a toast "Drink up" she said.

Whatever was in the cup was delicious and I was thirsty from the trip. I emptied my cup in a long continuous gulp.

Melanie watched with her mouth open in amazement, only when I had finished did she find her voice "Slow down, Honey" she laughed, "you won't last 'til dark at that rate"

"I was thirsty, and that hit the spot. What was it?"

"Dunmore punch" she replied "Mostly rum, with some fruit juice, coconut milk, and honey".

I saw her smiling expression falter for a moment as she noticed the overnight bag, but she quickly recovered her demeanor as she continued on in her adopted role of a tour guide.

"Dunmore Town is named after the Earl of Dunmore, who was once the Governor of Virginia, and who later became the Governor of the Bahamas in 1786. This was a ship building center and ships were built here up until 1922, the largest being the four-masted *Marie J. Thompson*. Many pirates lived here and the infamous Calico Jack once burned the town and a few fishing boats. Now the island is the home of 'the rich and famous' who come here to escape and to enjoy the world's finest beach".

"Thank you for the interesting information" I said politely, "now can we get away from all these people?"

A small crowd had gathered to listen to her spiel, obviously believing that she was an actual tour guide.

"I did this for a whole season, about 8 years ago".

"You're a natural".

"Where to, sir?" she asked.

"You're the guide, drive on" I ordered.

Today she was dressed for the beach, a bikini top and a pair of white shorts, no shoes, and no makeup. The golf cart she was driving was painted pink with little blue tassels around the roof.

"Nice buggy!" I commented.

"It's my Mummy's".

Another peculiarity of the Bahamians that I had noticed was the manner in which they referred to their parents. It was always Mummy and Daddy, never Mum and Dad, or Ma and Pa. It was strange to my ears, but then who's to say it's not correct.

"Where are we going?" I asked as she turned right after leaving the dock area.

"First we'll visit the Artist's Colony where many of the locals enjoy painting. They come down to the waters edge, set up their easels and paint the scenic panorama of the boats at anchor, the water birds and the sunset".

"Do you paint?" I asked.

"Only walls and fences" she answered with a smile.

"No sunsets?"

"I've never had the time or the patience. How about you?"

"Me neither, not even fences".

As she had predicted, off to our right there was a group of painters busily following their chosen occupation. We stopped to survey their work, several of the paintings were of the same scene, but the artist's individuality had made them all quite distinct from one another.

"I'm impressed" I said.

"There's a gallery in town, that we'll visit later, that sells the best of their work".

"Maybe I'll purchase one for a souvenir"

"Wait until you see the prices" she cautioned.

Just past the Artist's Colony was Valentine's Marina, where an impressive array of private yachts was moored. There were yachts of many sizes, some were much bigger than the Bohengy, and while they all looked immaculately maintained, I noticed that several of the crews were busy polishing and buffing to keep them up to snuff.

"This is more my style" I joked.

"Let's take a closer look" Melanie suggested as she parked the buggy in a cool place under a tree.

We walked along the docks inspecting the various vessels. It seemed that the further we went, the larger the yachts became.

"That's my favorite" Melanie sighed "It's so beautiful".

She was looking at a Broward Motor Yacht that was, by my reckoning, about a hundred and twenty five feet in length. Her name was 'Princess', and I had visions of the owner buying it for his mistress or maybe his daughter, certainly not his wife.

"I wonder who owns it?" I asked.

"People from Nassau" she replied, "the Boskos, a very wealthy family from Nassau, they made a fortune building Atlantis, I hear".

"Do you know them?"

"No, not really, I met one of the sons once at a party here. They own a lot of hotels in Nassau, plus they are one of the largest building contractors in the Bahamas".

"Let's see if we can get invited on board" I said.

"How?"

"You'll see, just play along".

We walked along the dock next to the boat, a member of the crew, dressed in tailored whites inquired as to whether he could be of assistance.

"Is Mr. Bosko on board?" I asked, with some authority.

"Yes sir, he is. Can I tell him whose calling?"

"David, from England, we met in Europe, tell him".

"One moment, please".

Melanie was having a fit. She was having trouble trying to keep her composure, but was enjoying my bravado. The crew man returned.

"Mr. Bosko will be right out, sir".

"Thank you very much. You keep her in beautiful shape" I said admiringly.

A moment later a small gray haired man appeared at the rail. I assumed that it must be Mr. Bosko.

"Hello" I called, "do you remember me, we met in Monte Carlo I think it was, or it could have been Nice, a couple of seasons ago?"

He looked confused, as I knew he would.

"Come on up". He beckoned us aboard.

"I'm David, this is my attorney Melanie" I explained.

We shook hands as he invited us into the spacious lounge. It was spectacular; I had to attract Melanie's attention to stop her gawking in awe at her surroundings.

"Would you care for a drink?" he asked.

"Bit early for us" I answered, "we've got a business lunch to attend later, best to keep a clear head".

"Of course"

"Tell me" I inquired in a quiet voice, "is she for sale?"

"Are you interested?" he asked.

"Yes, it would be convenient to have a yacht here, in addition to the one in Monte Carlo".

"Everything's for sale, at the right price" he replied nervously.

"And what is the right price, may I ask?"

"Eight" he answered dramatically.

"When was the keel laid?" I asked.

"Three years ago, 1999".

"Engines?"

"MTU's, twelve hundred each" he responded.

"Has she trans Atlantic range?"

"Yes, I had extra fuel tanks installed; she has a three thousand mile range at twelve knots".

"Perfect" I commented, "thank you so much for giving us the tour. She's lovely. I'll let you know".

We left Mr. Bosko in a state of bewilderment, walked back to our pink buggy, and went into Valentines bar for a well deserved drink.

Melanie could hold her composure no longer, as soon as we were out of ear shot, she burst into loud infectious laughter.

"I can't believe we did that" she giggled, "you were so convincing. He was totally sucked in. What did he mean by eight?'

"Million" I answered "dollars".

"I would have guessed much higher. That was so much fun"

"And no harm done" I added.

Melanie linked her arm through mine, "You're quite a guy, I'm not sure I'll be able to trust you. I could hardly believe my ears when you turned down a drink, saying it was too early, he must have smelled the rum on your breath. We both smell like a brewery"

We finished our drinks and ordered two more.

"I'd like to go for a swim" I suggested "I'm hot and sticky".

"I know the perfect place" she said.

The pink sand beach on Harbour Island's Atlantic side is world famous, and for good reason. As our buggy crested the top of the cliffs, we overlooked the miles of the spectacular pink sand beach that was almost deserted at this time of day. The view was inspiring. Melanie directed my attention to the south where she pointed to the land on the horizon which, she explained, was the mainland of Eleuthera. I could see a coral reef breaking the surface of the turquoise water some yards offshore, and a lone horseman riding bareback through the surf. It was breathtaking.

Melanie stripped off her shorts and ran down the beach to the water. "Come on" she called.

There was no one around, so while her back was to me, I quickly changed and followed her into the water.

"Nice tan" she laughed, as she jumped onto my back and wrestled me under the water.

I returned the favour after I recovered, picked her up and dunked her, making her cry out for mercy. I let her up carefully, only to be pulled back under again as she grabbed my legs and lifted me over her shoulders. She was as slippery as an eel, totally uninhibited with no modesty or shyness. She grabbed my swim suit at the back and pulled it down to my knees, then gave a huge kick and swam out towards the coral. I chased her, but I was no match to her adeptness in the water.

"I'll get you for that"

"You've gotta catch me first" she shrieked.

I slowly swam towards her, and then I stopped and winced with pain as I feigned a cramp. I knew that she had noticed. She paused in her endeavor to escape my pursuit, and came to help me. As she came close, I grabbed her around the waist and held her head under water. She kicked and struggled but I wouldn't release her, she reached around and squirmed between my legs, then reached up and grabbed me where she new it would hurt. She was free at last.

"That wasn't fair" she coughed "I thought you were hurt"

"I am now!" I complained.

"Serves you right"

"Truce?"

"I don't know if I can trust you".

"I'll be good, I promise".

We continued to play in the ocean like two kids, we were the only couple in the water, and I couldn't remember the last time that I had so much fun with anyone. Melanie was an absolute delight, always ready to explore any new idea, and completely captivated by my company. Maybe she's like this with everybody, I thought, she must have an older brother, because she wasn't shy about pulling up close to me whenever the occasion presented itself, and with the skimpiness of her swim suit, it was becoming hard for me to retain my control. I'm sure she was aware of the effect that she was having on me, in fact she was enjoying the whole experience.

"Is it lunch time yet?" I asked "I'm hungry".

"Me too".

"Where shall we go?"

"Right there" she said as she pointed to a place off to our left, "that's Coral Sands; we can go just the way we are".

"I need to find some money" I said.

"OK, I'll meet you there".

I went to the buggy, retrieved my wallet from my shorts, gathered up our towels and walked over to the outdoor restaurant that Melanie had chosen.

She saw the towels I was carrying.

"Am I embarrassing you?" she asked, "d'you want me to cover up?"

"Not at all" I lied "I thought you might want to dry off".

"Thank you" she whispered, "you're so thoughtful".

There were several other patrons in the restaurant, most were dressed, none were as undressed as we were. Anyway nobody knows me here, I thought, so why not enjoy the local style. A waitress came to take our food order; we hadn't even glanced at the menus that had been placed on our table.

"Give us a few moments?" I asked, "but we will have a drink".

"A Bahamian Surprise" Melanie ordered.

"And I'll have a Bloody Mary. This is a nice place" I said, after the waitress had left, "do you come here often?"

"Only when I'm entertaining rich male clients".

"I noticed that everyone knows you".

"This is a small island, everyone knows everyone, I went to school with that waitress".

"I'll let you decide on lunch".

"The Grouper is usually good".

"Then Grouper it is".

The food was outstanding, the ambiance was wonderful, the temperature was pleasantly cool under the striped awning, and the company was unequalled. I felt liked I died and gone to heaven. I was relishing every moment, wondering when I would wake up and find that I was dreaming. I pinched myself to be sure that I was awake.

"What are you doing?" she asked.

"Just checking to be sure that I wasn't dreaming. This is so fantastic; nobody will believe me when I tell them. I'm so glad we met".

"I'm glad too. It's a pity we can't stay here forever".

"I can".

"No you can't. You have a family, obligations and responsibilities".

I was enjoying my rebellious thoughts, even considering the possibility of making a dramatic change in the direction of my life, when I felt two hands clamp down hard on my shoulders. I was startled back to reality.

"David, David I can't believe it's you. What the hell are you doing here?"

I turned to look to see who was gripping me so hard. It was Charlie Wolfsen.

"Charlie" I stammered with surprise, "this is quite a shock".

"What are you up to?"

"I'm here on vacation" I answered.

"Bullshit" he answered, "you're here for a reason, you can't fool me".

"Honestly, I am. I'm sorry; this is Melanie, my lawyer".

"You're a scoundrel David, lawyer indeed. You must think I'm crazy if you expect me to believe that" he said, as he punched me in the back.

"Anyway, more to the point, what are you doing here?" I asked.

"Me. I live here. I have a house here. On the beach, about 200 yards that way". He said pointing in what I think was north.

"In fact" he continued "why don't you come by for a drink, stay for dinner, meet some of my friends. Then you can tell me what you're really doing here. Bring your lawyer with you".

He paused to smile at his own attempt at humour. "Where are you staying?"

"In Spanish Wells" I replied.

"You must be kidding" he laughed, as he repeated to himself "Spanish Wells. David you always were a kidder. How about it, come on up to the house when you've finished lunch"

"We only have these clothes" I apologized.

"They're fine. We'll all be outside at the pool. I'll see you in awhile. You can't miss the house; it's called Shangri La, just follow the road to the right".

And then he was gone.

"A good friend of yours?" inquired Melanie.

"More of a business acquaintance than a friend, although we were close friends a long time ago" I answered "I've worked with him in the past".

"He's English, right?"

"Very much so. He's a rich man, and spends his money like water. Do you know the house?"

"It's a huge place. I've always wanted to go inside".

"Well, now's your chance. I'm not sure I want to stay for dinner though, let's play it by ear".

"That's fine. I hope I won't be out of place".

"There'll be lots of pretty girls there, I can guarantee that. Charlie surrounds himself with beautiful things and gorgeous women".

"Then I'd better keep a close eye on you" she laughed.

"Don't worry, you'll be the prettiest one there" I said gallantly.

"Well, thank you kind sir".

After lunch, we decided to have a snooze on a couple of chaises on the beach. I pulled them into the shade beneath an umbrella. Melanie stretched her towel over the plastic webbing and settled into a deep sleep. I stayed awake thinking about Charlie Wolfsen. Of all the people in the world that I had met, Charlie was one of my favorites. I'd heard that in business he was ruthless, but in his dealings with me, he had always been beyond reproach. We went back a long way, before he became a multi millionaire, in fact I could remember a time when I had actually loaned him a few quid. To think that here on this remote island I would encounter Charlie. It must be fate. Sleep finally over took me, as I succumbered to my fatigue and the grouper.

Shangri La was all that the name implied, an oasis of wealth and opulence, nestled among a grove of palms and overlooking the long sandy beach of Harbour Island. Charlie greeted us to his 'modest home', his actual words, led us through the manicured grounds to the rear of the house, to where a group of seven or eight of the chosen people were gathered.

53

Charlie introduced us to his friends while continuing to hold on to my arm.

"Everyone" he called "this is one of my dearest friends, David and I go back many years, more than I care to remember, I still can't believe that he's here".

There was something for everyone. A continuous parade of waiters offered all kinds of snacks, while the champagne flowed like water; even the music was a perfect, a mixture of rock, oldies and sentimental ballads. Good old Charlie, he certainly knew how to entertain.

I took Melanie's hand and escorted her to the pool, where most of the guests had congregated "Don't get lost" I told her "or propositioned".

She squeezed my hand, "Don't forget about me".

"I won't, but if I disappear for a while, it'll probably mean that I'm with Charlie".

"As long as it's only Charlie" she warned "I've never seen such beautiful girls, they look like models or movie stars".

"Most likely they are" I answered "Charlie's big in the entertainment business. These girls are most likely on his payroll".

"What about the men?"

"People he's trying to impress".

"This is like something out of a movie, I feel so ordinary".

"You're the only one here with a brain; these girls would give anything to be like you".

As the day wore on, we became conditioned to Charlie's extravagance. It was easy to relax and enjoy the surroundings, the fun people, the constant supply of refreshments and Charlie's exuberance.

"You will stay for dinner?" Charlie pleaded.

"I won't need any dinner if you don't stop serving all these delicious hors d'ouvres" I replied.

"It's just a cook out, steaks and the like. Nothing too fancy".

"Charlie" I said "You can't do anything that isn't fancy. I'll bet you've flown the steaks in from Scotland; there'll be Maine Lobster, Scampi and all sorts of unusual accompaniments".

"Your lawyer friend seems to be enjoying herself".

"She fits in anywhere she goes, and she really is a lawyer".

"Whatever you say. Now you will stay, I won't take no for an answer. And I want you stay over, both of you, there's plenty of room".

"I dunno Charlie, this is our first date, plus I'm married, in case you've forgotten".

"How could I ever forget, you married the one girl I always wanted. Stay in separate rooms, I don't care. But I want to talk to you after dinner".

"I'll talk to Melanie, I'll let her decide".

As I had predicted, Melanie had become the center of attraction at the pool, her natural beauty and easy going manner had endeared her to the phony girls. She was enjoying her new found role, relating stories of her early life in Harbour Island, and of her driving ambition to become a highly qualified lawyer. She excused herself from her admirers, when she saw me trying to attract her attention, she really was beautiful and I felt very proud in the knowledge that she was with me, as I watched her hurry to where I was standing.

"Having a good time?"

"Yes, but they ask so many questions".

"I'm sure you know why?"

"I know that I'm different to the girls they normally meet in their everyday lives, but you wouldn't believe some of the things they want to know".

"Like what?"

"I'm too embarrassed to tell you".

"Sexual things?'

"Yes, and details, you just can't imagine".

"Goes to show how shallow they are, they're only topic of conversation is sex".

"Where have you been?"

"With Charlie. He insists that I stay the night; he invited you to stay as well. I told him that I'd relay his invitation; he says that there are plenty of rooms. We can share or each have our own."

"I don't know what to say".

"Let me tell you what I think".

"Ok".

"I hope you don't misunderstand me, but I think that you should go home. Remember, this is your home, people think very highly of you on this Island, to some people you're a role model. You shouldn't jeopardize your reputation by accepting this invitation. Much as I would like you to!"

Melanie reached up and kissed me. The look in her misty eyes scared me; I'd seen that look before, a long time ago. "Thank you" she whispered "We'll have another chance sometime, I hope".

"Stay for the cook out, and then slip away" I suggested.

"Will I see you tomorrow?"

"You bet you will. I'll see you in church in the morning, then we'll have lunch at the Harbour Lodge".

"I feel better all ready" she smiled.

Charlie's simple back yard barbeque took on the form of a gourmet grill-a-thon, nothing was missing, there was something to satisfy even the most refined taste along with more ordinary fare. For some reason, I was hungry; it could have been the tantalizing aromas, the sea air, or the result of the frolicking that Melanie and I had enjoyed in the morning. We both consumed too much, and vowed to start watching our respective weights in the future.

"I'm ready to leave. I'll be right back, after I say goodbye to Charlie" Melanie said.

"Do you want me to come with you?"

"No, I'll find him".

She went into the house to look for our host. I considered the merits of the tough decision that I had made. I know it was the correct course of action, and as she had said, there would be more opportunities in the future. Maybe, maybe not. Melanie was back in next to no time, she waved goodbye to the glamorous ensemble of models and actresses, then she walked to where I was sitting.

"I'll walk you to the buggy" I offered.

"Let's go" she answered.

We both felt a little sad that this unforgettable day was coming to an abrupt end, and not the end that either of us had had in mind. I took her hand as we strolled along the driveway to the pink buggy.

"Quite a day" I reflected.

"It was almost perfect" she commented.

"I know, I feel badly about the way it's ended".

"I'm glad that I told you to bring your tooth brush" she grinned "At least you'll get to use it".

"I would rather have used it at your sink".

"Another time. And I will see you tomorrow".

Farewells are not one of my strong suits. She was standing beside the buggy ready for me to change my mind and whisk her off to some romantic hide away. I couldn't, at least not now. I opened my arms and she came to me with her lips apart, we kissed passionately for a brief moment.

"Get going, before I change my mind" I said softly "You're too tempting".

"Until tomorrow" she cooed "And thank you for a wonderful day".

The party was winding down when I returned. Charlie called to me to join him for a night cap. We both collected a snifter of brandy from the bar, then retreated into the library.

"So" he started off, "are you going to tell me why you are here?"

"Just like I told you, I'm on vacation".

"David, I know you as well as I know anyone in this world, and I know you're hiding something. You're up to something, maybe you did come here on vacation, although I find that hard to believe, but now there's something on your mind. And it's not just the girl".

He reached over to the table where he had deposited the bottle of brandy, and without asking poured a generous amount into both of our glasses. I could tell by his expression that he was going to reminisce about our past times together; it was a pattern that I had come to recognize over the years; give him some good brandy after a hectic day, and he would reach back into his memory to find an interesting anecdote that would endear you to him forever.

"Do you remember that time we got a lift in that ice cream truck?" he grinned, "it was one of our funniest times together".

"I'll never forget. I think I may still have some of the bruises".

Charlie and I had been returning to London along the old A4 highway, we'd been to Devon on a business venture that went sour; we were close to Salisbury when our transmission failed. It was a Sunday evening, and the chance of us finding a garage that was even open, let alone having a mechanic who could fix the problem was slim to none. We were stuck on the side of the road considering our options, when a van stopped to help. Charlie and I were dressed in business suits complete with white shirts and ties and to the van driver and his buddy, I'm sure we looked like two helpless office types that they could take advantage of, or who would pay dearly for a ride into London.

We accepted their offer of a ride, locked our car, and placed a notice in the window to tell the police that we would be calling a garage first thing in the morning to have it towed; then we clambered into the back of the van. The driver closed the door and pulled away in a hurry, sending us both sliding across the floor of the truck and landing us in a heap in the corner. The inside of the van was as smooth as the proverbial baby's bottom, there was nothing to hold on to, not a corner molding, a window ledge, or a door frame, there was nothing at all, and each time that the van turned or slowed down, we were thrown around like two rag dolls. We banged on the cab wall to get the attention of the driver but all our banging went unheeded, in fact it was my guess that the two morons up front were enjoying every moment. There was a small skylight in the roof that provided a sliver of light and a little fresh air. After twenty minutes of this torture, I started to see the funny side of our predicament, and Charlie had gone from being mad, to being scared, to being resigned to the fact that we were trapped. I watched as he slid on his back from side to side of the interior of the van, eventually colliding with me in a jumble of arms and legs. I started to laugh, after a moment Charlie joined in, and then we couldn't stop. We were like a pair of kids giggling uncontrollably as the van continued on its way to London. We both hurt from the bruising impacts with each other and with the walls of the van, but I believe that I hurt more from the laughing than from the battering.

Eventually the van came to a stop, the rear door was flung open, and four hands grabbed us and dragged us into a ditch. We were too tired and too weak to put up much of a fight, but I did land a good kick on one of our tormentors as he scrambled into the driver's cab. Then the van was gone.

I looked at Charlie as he lay on his back in the ditch, he was still laughing. It had started to drizzle with rain, and unnoticed by either one of us, we had picked up a coating of a white powder from the inside of the van. I don't know if it was flour or confectioner's sugar, but with the addition of the rain it became extremely sticky. The contents of the ditch were now stuck to us, leaves, grass and dirt covered us from head to toe, and that was when the police car arrived.

"I'll never forget the look on that copper's face when you told him that you were a friend of Prime Minister" I giggled.

"And that you were acquainted with a chief inspector at Scotland Yard", Charlie added.

"I wonder what ever became of those two drivers?"

"I never told you?" declared Charlie "I tracked down the company they worked for, and bought it, and then had those two morons transferred to one of the worst locations in the country".

"Really? I never knew".

I looked at my watch in the hope that Charlie would take the hint and suggest that we called it a day, but instead he poured more brandy into our glasses.

"That was quite the spread you put on today" I commented, "how do you bring in all the fresh food?"

"I have a plane. It's tied up on the bay side, it's a float plane. Just perfect for a place like this".

"Could I ask you for a favour?"

"Anything. You know that".

"Could you have the plane fly to Spanish Wells on Thursday at 8.30 in the morning, to make a pick up?"

"To pick up what?"

"Fish" I answered.

"Is this some kind of joke?"

"No, let me explain. I met this very nice fella on Spanish Wells, he says he's Canadian but from his accent I'm sure that he's a Brit from London. Anyway he's raising fish on a farm, and needs to get a hundred pounds of fresh fish to his customer in Florida, and since you have a plane that's going to Florida, I thought we could help him".

"I knew you were up to something, David, I just knew. Since when do you help total strangers?"

"Maybe I've changed".

"Come on! Who do you think you're kidding? What's really going on the plane? Drugs?"

"No, absolutely not. Just two forty pound boxes of fresh fish".

"Fresh fish, eh?"

"I give you my word, that's all it is".

"Then there has to be something else, a reason that you're not telling me? Come on David, what's going on?"

"Ok" I told him "I need a diversion".

"A diversion? You're going to load two boxes of fish on my plane on Thursday morning and have it flown to Florida as a diversion. A diversion from what?"

"Not exactly a diversion, more of a decoy".

I knew that I would have to tell Charlie my plan. I was trying to decide how much of my plan I needed to tell him.

"I'm going to rob the bank in Spanish Wells", I stated calmly.

"Of what, the church funds?"

"Not exactly" I said, "in fact it's more like 10 million".

"No way" he shouted, "not in Spanish Wells, there's not that much money in that little place".

"Charlie, do you think that I'm stupid! I 'm telling you there is, or there will be on Wednesday".

"You'd better tell me the whole story".

"Next week the fishing boats will return with their catch of crawfish tails, most of the boats will be in by Friday and the packing plant will buy all the catch. Charlie, I've watched them, they get paid in cash, green backs, moula, or whatever you want to call it, lots and lots of it. Right there under our noses."

"You've checked this out?"

"Of course I have. The bank brings in the money on Wednesday, so that it has enough cash on hand for all the fishermen to be paid. Next week they are bringing in 10 million dollars. I've checked. The money will stay in the bank until Friday morning".

"But you're going to remove it on Thursday?"

"That's the plan".

Charlie was thinking, I know he respected my professional assessment, but he was having a hard time figuring out how I was going to pull this off.

"The money will all be in Bahamian Dollars" he stated triumphantly, thinking that he had found a flaw in my plan.

"Of course it will" I agreed, "that's why the bank is so lax in their protection".

"You've cased the bank?"

"It's a piece of cake, maybe the easiest job I've ever had. There are only four or five employees, no

63

guards, no alarms and the building is not really built as a bank. It's just a conventional two storey building that the bank rents from a man in Nassau, in fact there's an apartment above the bank. The bank even has a bathroom on an outside wall, a kid could break in!"

"Ok, so you grab the money, these Bahamian dollars, that have no value outside the Bahamas, then what?"

"The less you know the better" I said, "just be sure your plane lands on the water at the East end of the island early Thursday morning".

"OK, OK, the plane will be there. I knew that you came here for a reason".

"I didn't Charlie, I came to relax for a while, but I saw all the cash being exchanged and I couldn't resist".

We were both tired from the long day's activities, so we decided against having another drink and made our way upstairs to the bedrooms.

"I know I won't sleep for wondering how you're gonna convert the cash" said Charlie.

"I'll tell you after it's done. I might need your help later on in my plan".

CHAPTER FOUR

Sunday morning crept in from the East across the ocean, the early morning sky slowly lightened as dawn caressed the low clouds, turning them into wondrously illuminated forms whose shapes changed continuously as the morning breeze herded them like cattle, into a tight knot on the horizon. It was peaceful to be on the beach at dawn. I had come down earlier to sleep under the stars, to reflect and capture a glimpse of my inner self, and to try to understand what part of me it was that pushed and prodded the roguish side of my make up.

I was a relatively happy man with the financial capability of continuing the high life style that both my family and I had come to enjoy. So it wasn't the money that motivated me. I was discontent, without a reason that I could put my finger on. I had this feeling that I'd missed something in my life, yet from an outsiders perspective I had achieved the dream that many envied. My pursuit and conquest of Melanie, was unfair to several people, those I would not intentionally hurt, those that I loved, and of course to Melanie herself.

Yet here I was preparing to continue with the flirtation and to relish every minute. If I had a voice inside which I paid heed to, it would have warned me to stop, to resist, to be a more honest individual, but I have no such voice or I had learned how to turn a deaf ear to it. Knowing all these weaknesses in my nature should have made me sad or repentative, but the fact was it made me feel superior, and I knew that I would continue as long as I could get away with it. It takes a scoundrel to know one.

One of the quirks of my nature is that I genuinely care about people and am highly considerate of their feelings, yet by contrast I use people and take advantage of them. A case in point is Melanie. I know that she thinks that she's in love with me, I remember only to well that expression in her eyes when she left last night, and while I know that I'm not in love with her, I do have more than a casual interest in her. Am I flattered by her attention? Do I care what happens to her? Will we remain friends, if not lovers, when this caper is over? The answer to all those questions is, yes!

I avoided Charlie and his entourage of hangers on; I didn't feel like listening to their mundane conversation so early in the day. I showered, shaved, preened myself a little, borrowed a gray suit from Charlie's huge wardrobe, then quietly escaped from the house.

I slung the suit jacket over my shoulder and walked through town to the church, trying to stay cool and composed.

The church that I had seen the previous day when riding in the pink buggy with Melanie was adjacent to the main square. It was old, built of limestone in the standard British architectural style. The doors were open wide, and a large crowd was congregated outside as families and friends greeted one another. I was glad that I had had the foresight to borrow one of Charlie's suits, as the assembly of people was dressed in their finery. The ladies wore incredible hats, of weird designs and loud colours. Ascot, on Derby day, was nothing compared to this!

I couldn't see Melanie, and for a moment I thought that maybe she had come to her senses and had decided not to attend church today, or her family had told her not to make a fool of herself and to forget her association with this strange foreigner. I was on the verge of walking away from the church, when I felt an arm slip under my arm, I turned to greet her. She was stunningly dressed in a pink dress that ended several inches above her knees. She must have been poured into the dress as there was no way that it could have slid over her. A small hat and veil completed her outfit. I held her at arms length to take it all in.

"You look beautiful" I said, "Halle Berry move over!"

"You look nice too".

I was surprised that she was alone; I had expected to meet a few members of her family. She explained that they attended the Methodist church and that was the reason she was almost late, as she had dropped them of first before continuing on here.

If I had been asked, I would have described the morning service as interesting, every seat was occupied and the congregation was highly vocal in the rendition of the hymns. I was pleasantly surprised to find that I knew most of the words of three out of the five hymns that had been selected. The last time that I had attended church was nineteen years ago when I was married. My family and friends were liberally minded enough to understand that regular attendance at church did not necessarily enhance ones chances of entering heaven, or even produce a person with Christian values. I have several acquaintances that are devoted to their local church and attend on a regular basis, but in their everyday lives they are hypocrites, gossips and quite dishonest; it has become a trait of mine in business to prefer to deal with those people who do not set themselves up high on a lofty pedestal, or believe that they are on a higher spiritual level than me. I just don't trust self righteous Christians; I rather deal with 'normal' crooks.

The sermon had a message that was directed specifically towards me, it was uncanny. The biblical references that the preacher quoted could have been selected by my wife, every word he chanted drove another arrow into my heart. I really was a sinner; but then I've always known that!

I stood proudly for the singing of the final hymn, it was a favorite of mine and I sang with a gusto that surprised me, and those seated in the adjacent pews.

"You were in fine voice today" Melanie said as we exited the church.

"I like to sing, you should here me in the shower some time" I said.

"I'd love to" she said coyly.

"I didn't mean literally, it was just an expression".

"Don't be defensive; I'm a big girl you know".

"I'm well aware of that" I agreed as I passed my eyes over her with an exaggerated stare. "Are you hungry?" I asked, "I missed breakfast".

"Let me take you to my very favorite place for lunch, I already called to ask if they would let us in".

"Why wouldn't they, if it's a restaurant?'

"They only cater to their registered guests, but I have a friend who works there".

Melanie removed her hat, shook out her hair, and unbuttoned the top buttons of her dress in an attempt to make herself more comfortable. I followed her lead by removing my jacket and tie, and then we set off for lunch at Runaway Hill.

It was a small resort with a European influence situated on 5 acres of tropical gardens over looking the beach and the Atlantic Ocean. Spectacular could barely describe the place accurately; if ever I remarried this would be the place for my honeymoon. There were only 3 other couples in the small intimate dining room, they were all engrossed with each other and paid no attention to Melanie and me, as we entered and were seated close to the verandah, where we had a panoramic view of the beach.

"I can see why this is your favorite".

"I always wanted to stay here" she commented, "with the right person".

I didn't rise to the bait. I just nodded my head as I looked through the menu.

"See anything you fancy?" she asked.

"Plenty" I replied.

"What exactly do you want?" she inquired.

"I'll have whatever you have".

"How much time do we have?"

"Enough", I said.

"You're sure?" she said "I don't want to rush".

Ironically she ordered Crawfish Creole, and with every bite, I tasted apprehension mixed with a trace of fear. I could still forget my whole plan, stay here with

Melanie for a while, avoid the anxiety of the next few days, play it safe and be smart.

"You're very quiet" she observed.

"Sorry" I answered "I have something to ask you, and I'm not so sure that I should. It would mean that you would become involved with me in a business venture".

"I want to be involved", she answered eagerly.

"This is business, Melanie. You'll be acting as my lawyer".

"And your friend?"

"Yes. But our friendship could be jeopardized".

"Tell me what's on your mind".

"You're sure you want to know. If I tell you, and you decide that you don't want to be involved, it will be hard for me to trust you".

"Sounds very sinister".

"I want you to prepare the legal papers to purchase the 'Princess', Bosko's yacht!" I stated.

There was a silence that seemed to go on for five minutes before Melanie finally found her voice "You're serious; aren't you?"

"You bet I am, very serious", I replied.

"All right, tell me more. It's for Charlie; Right?"

I didn't answer her question, but proceeded to give her the details of the transaction.

"You'll need to prepare an Offer to Purchase document in the amount of eight million dollars. The offer is being made by the Olympus Corporation of 976, Gustav Boulevard, Geneva, Switzerland. Here, I've written the details down for you. The closing day is next Thursday, at Valentines Marina on an 'as is where is basis'. The full payment will be made in cash".

Melanie had her business face on as she listened attentively to me, she read the detailed note that I had given to her, she thought for a moment and then asked a series of questions.

"Who will sign for Olympus?"

"I will"

"We'll need a Corporate Resolution Form, giving you that authority".

"I have it" I commented.

"Are you waiving a survey?"

"Yes"

"And a sea trial?"

"Yes"

"Are there any conditions?"

"Such as?"

"Do you want to retain the crew? Do you want to take delivery here or in Nassau? Mr. Bosko may have several personal items that he will need to remove".

"If the crew wishes to stay, they can stay. I would like to travel with the yacht to Nassau on Thursday, give Bosko time to remove his belongings and collect anything that he may have there that belongs on board".

"Can I come along?" she grinned.

"As my lawyer?" I asked.

"As anything you would like me to be, lawyer, friend, companion, whatever".

By the time we had finished lunch and rehashed all the possible ramifications involved with the purchase of the 'Princess', it was time for me to return to the dock to board the Bohengy for the journey back to Spanish Wells.

Melanie had been a trifle subdued since she had learned of the planned purchase, I knew that she had probably figured out that her assumption that the yacht was for Charlie, was not entirely accurate. She was smart enough to realize that the paperwork that was required could not have been prepared ahead of time and that for me to have a Corporate Resolution already signed and available on such short notice was virtually impossible. She smelled a rat, but had decided to play along. She knew that she had nothing to lose and maybe she had something to gain. If nothing else it would be valuable experience.

We stopped briefly at Shangri La for me to return Charlie's suit, collect my over night bag, and say farewell. Charlie hugged me close and told me to stay in touch. He gave me a thumbs up sign, which I interpreted as having two meanings, first to indicate that he approved of Melanie, and secondly that the Thursday morning rendezvous was confirmed.

I decided to take Melanie into my confidence and to tell her about my plan. Not the heist part, but the plans for the yacht.

"You have my number in Spanish wells? If anything goes wrong with Bosko, make sure that you call me before Thursday".

"Nothing will go wrong! I'll see you back here Thursday morning as planned".

"Pack plenty of clothes" I said casually.

"Why? Just for a trip to Nassau?"

"I thought that you might like to accompany me on the next part of my trip?"

"To where?"

"Well" I explained "I'm sending the yacht to Bermuda, and you can go along for the ride, or you can join me".

"And where are you going?"

"Las Vegas".

"Oh, my God" she screamed "Las Vegas. Wow. Are you serious?"

"We'll stay in Nassau for a couple of days, and then fly out".

"For how long?"

"Maybe three days. There's a convention I have to attend".

"David, this is the most exciting thing that's ever happened to me. How long have you known about this trip?"

"A few days".

"And you kept it a secret from me? How do you keep all this bottled up inside of you? You must learn to share your thoughts. It's called communicating".

I laughed. If only she knew, I thought, but then what she didn't know wouldn't hurt her.

"So" I said, "from your reaction, I am to assume that the answer to my question is a yes".

"What question was that?"

"That you would like to accompany me, of course".

"Wild horses couldn't prevent me from going. Are you sure that you won't get bored with me" she said, as she snuggled closer and nibbled my ear.

"It's only for a few days" I replied, "any longer, and it could be a problem".

She pulled the buggy off to the side of the road, grabbed my head with both hands, pulled my face close to hers and gave me a long passionate kiss.

"I'll make sure that you don't get bored" she smiled.

It was time to leave, the ferry was boarding the last of the passengers, and the crew was preparing to cast off the docking lines.

"This is it. Time to go, I'll see you on Thursday".

"I can hardly wait" she cried, "thank you for having so much confidence in me, it means a lot to me".

We kissed tenderly, hugged each other one last time before I passed my ticket to be checked aboard. I watched as she continued to wave until the ferry was out of sight.

The trip back to Spanish Wells was uneventful, and as the ferry entered the narrow channel that led into the harbour, I had a feeling that I was returning home. The two days in Harbour Island had exhausted me and I was looking forward to a well deserved rest. There was no one to welcome me as I disembarked. I found my rented buggy and headed off to the Adventurers Hotel.

CHAPTER FIVE

At 8.30 Thursday morning I was sitting on board of Calhoun's Ferry boat waiting to be taken to the airport on North Eleuthera. The ferry boat was part of a 'package' trip of boat and taxi service to the airport that left from Pinders Supermarket about an hour or so prior to the various airlines departure times. My scheduled departure was at ten, hence my arrival on the boat at 8.30.

I heard the drone of a low flying plane, and stood to watch Charlie's float plane circle once, then descend to land at the east end of the island. A small power boat approached the plane and even from my less than ideal vantage point, I could see two men loading boxes on to the plane. I hoped that I wasn't the only witness to this morning activity, and a survey of the waterfront confirmed my suspicion that nothing went unobserved in this town. A group of men having coffee outside of Ronald Service Centre had seen the plane, two ferry boat operators were also witnesses, and there were probably many more.

The transfer of the cargo was completed in just a few moments, and then the plane revved its engines and flew away in a cloud of spray. Mission accomplished.

I had already returned my buggy to Pinders Rentals, checked out of the hotel, and packed the 8 million dollars into two Igloo coolers, that were now, together with the rest of my bags, on board Calhoun's ferry.

As I had predicted, the robbery had been a piece of cake. It was completed in less than 15 minutes; there were no interruptions, no surprises, no hidden alarms and no witnesses. I had purchased two coolers from the Islander Shop, and had made a noticeable fuss about filling them with crawfish to take with me when I left. For two days I had made myself conspicuous by driving the buggy with the Igloos on the seat, I was so noticeable that I became a part of the scenery and conveniently slipped out of people's memories.

I left two million behind at the bank, as a gesture of my good upbringing, I had been taught not to be greedy. I had replaced the bundles of bank notes with several phone directories, and then I had spread the remaining 2 million over the books. The purpose of this subterfuge was to buy a little extra time; I was convinced that the missing money would not be noticed until Friday, when the bank prepared for the large withdrawal by the seafood wholesaler. If one of the bank's employees happened to move the box containing the money and notice that the weight was not right, then they might make an inspection and discover the loss at an earlier time.

On Tuesday night I had made a dry run. At four in the morning I had driven my buggy to the bank and parked on its western side close to the emergency generator room. I had turned off the engine, restarted it a couple of times to create a realistic noise, coughed and cleared my throat several times, made enough noise to wake the dead, yet still I went undetected. The town was fast asleep.

If my calculations were proven to be correct, and the robbery was not discovered until Friday, then my escape would be complete. I would be in Nassau by Thursday afternoon and on my way to Vegas early on Friday. The 'money' would be on its way to Bermuda, already converted into an internationally negotiable asset.

Calhoun piloted the ferry to Jeans Bay, the closest point on the mainland of Eleuthera to Spanish Wells, where he kept a mini van that he used to transport his passengers to the airport. He helped me lift my coolers of 'crawfish' out of the boat and into the van.

"These are heavy. How much crawfish do you have?" he asked.

"About fifty pounds" I answered "the rest is ice. It's the ice that's heavy".

At the airport we unloaded my bags and the coolers from the taxi. Calhoun disappeared into the terminal to check on the daily flights that would be bringing passengers for him to convey to Spanish Wells. I saw him deep in a conversation with several of the airline employees; he was having breakfast with them and seemed to be occupied. I hailed a taxi from the several that were close by, quickly loaded my bags and the coolers inside and directed the driver to Harbour Island. Nobody paid any attention to my change of plan, or to the baggage that I was carrying. The taxi connected with another small ferry boat for the final stage of the trip to Valentines.

The purchase of the yacht was completed quickly. Melanie had performed her work perfectly, there were no hitches, all the paperwork was completed and I had a signed and notarized bill of sale in my hot little hand within the hour. I had breathed an inaudible sigh of relief. Within an hour of my arrival the yacht slipped its moorings and began its voyage to Nassau. In preparation for the trip, the Captain had hired the services of a local pilot for the transit through the Devil's Backbone. I only had a moment to escape from the bridge as I recognized the pilot as he came aboard. It was Little Willy. I did not want him to see me. There was only a remote possibility that he might mention my presence on the yacht to Calhoun, but it was a chance that I could not afford to take. I went below to the master stateroom, telling Bosko that I was feeling queasy and was going to lie down.

Melanie knocked on the door and called, "are you all right?"

"I'm fine" I answered, "come on in".

"Are you seasick?"

"No, I'm fine. I just needed to be alone for a while".

"Do you want me to leave?"

"Of course not. In case I forgot to mention it, you did a very professional job today. You handled the whole transaction perfectly. I'm proud of you".

"As you would say, 'it was a piece of cake'" she joked.

I felt the engines slow and realized that we were entering the main entrance channel to Spanish Wells, soon the pilot would be gone and I would feel totally safe. I watched as the town passed by, and felt a touch of nostalgia even though I had only been a temporary resident. I'd become attached to the place and its terrific people.

Ever since that first day when I had set foot on Spanish Wells I had been seeking answers to a multitude of questions that were related to the community and its unique status in the Bahamas. It was while I was standing in line at the bank listening to the customer's conversations, that I found an answer that satisfied me.

I was reminded of Milk Wood, the imaginary town portrayed so beautifully in the play written by that master of the English language, Dylan Thomas. He describes in his play for voices, a complete day in Milk Wood, from dawn to dusk, through a collection of characters with fictitious names that pertained to their various occupations. The characters were brought to life by a cast of Welsh actors in a production produced for the BBC in London.

The characters of Spanish Wells are of the same ilk, but unlike the Dylan Thomas characters that were fictitious; those of Spanish Wells are real. Mr. Sands, who lives on the beach; Mrs. Cash, who dispenses money in the bank; Fred Digger, who works in the cemetery; Emma Stamp, who works at the Post Office; Mrs. Sweeting, the confectioner; Mr. Lowe, who sings baritone in the church choir and Mr. Sawyer the carpenter.

And as each day closes and the next day opens, the people of Spanish Wells blossom, reveling in their independence and lifting their metaphorical arms in a heart felt salutation to their maker.

I made a mental note to send a copy of the Dylan Thomas book 'Under Milk Wood' and a recording of the radio broadcast to the local school.

Two weeks ago I had made the trip from Nassau to Spanish Wells on board the Bohengy, now I was making the return trip on my own luxury yacht in the company of a delightful, sexy young lady. It had been an eventful time, totally unexpected, and so unbelievable that I had a difficult time in grasping the enormity of what I had achieved. The plan was to tie up at the Nassau Harbour Club for the night, to allow Bosko to remove the contents of the closets and a pair of ugly pictures that he valued. I noticed that he had very few personal possessions, and thought that he was a little like me in that regard, both of us living as if tomorrow could be our last day on earth.

The crew of the 'Princess' consisted of the Captain, and three deckhands, one of whom was a girl and the others were sorta male. The girl, who's name was Sandy, introduced herself to us and produced a bottle of champagne from the galley. She filled two crystal glasses with the cold bubbly and made a toast to the new owner and his wife!

Melanie's eyes found mine, as she quickly blurted out, "we're not married".

Sandy was embarrassed and blushed as she made her apology.

"That's all right" I said, "a natural mistake. I'm actually rather flattered".

"Join us?" invited Melanie, "if you'd like to?"

"Maybe another time. I've got chores to attend to" she replied.

I carried the champagne out onto the aft deck, where there was a selection of comfortable reclining chairs. I selected a swinging love seat, knowing that Melanie would join me. She needed no invitation and she never played games; it was another one of her many attributes that I loved.

"This is like something out of a movie" she said.

"You're repeating yourself".

"I know, but I still can't believe that I'm here. With you. On this fabulous yacht. On my way to Vegas. It's all a wonderful dream and I don't want to wake up".

"It's all true. I think it's just great, I could become used to this life quite easily".

"What shall we do tonight?" she asked.

"Where would you like to go?"

"Somewhere romantic, where the music is unobtrusive, somewhere where we can smooch a little".

I wanted to say "I know just the place" but I didn't, so I said that we could ask when we reached Nassau.

"I brought a long dress with me; maybe I can wear it tonight?"

"There's a place named Greycliffe. It's a five star restaurant, we could have dinner there, and then go dancing later if you'd like".

"Oh yes, it's supposed to be wonderful there, but I'm sure we'll need a reservation".

I lifted the intercom telephone from its cradle on the wicker table. Instantly the Captain responded.

"Would you be kind enough to make a reservation for us at Greycliffe, eight o'clock should be Ok".

I replaced the receiver. I looked across to Melanie and we both burst into laughter.

Just as we regained our composure the telephone rang, it was the Captain.

"I'm sorry, sir" he said politely "Greycliffe is closed for renovations, but I have taken the liberty of making a reservation at the Paradise Island Harbour Club, I'm sure that you will enjoy it"

"Thank you very much, I appreciate your thoughtfulness".

I relayed this information to Melanie.

"I'm sure it will be fine" she said "I think the Captain knows his way around and he wouldn't dare steer his new boss wrong".

The 'Princess' was equipped with the latest in electronic equipment, including a world wide satellite telephone system. It would be so easy to call home, to tell Laura and Annie to meet me in Nassau, but how would I explain this new acquisition, I meant the yacht not Melanie. They wouldn't want to understand, they were content with their lives as they were. I suppose that was one of the problems in our marriage. Living on the edge just didn't cut it for a person doomed to have responsibilities.

"Penny for your thoughts" said Melanie.

"Sorry, I was miles away"

"I could see that".

"Without revealing your true feelings, Melanie, what is it that you find attractive about me?"

"I could answer that question, by asking you a question".

"Such as?"

"Why do you need to know? I wouldn't have thought that you were insecure?"

"I suppose I was doing a little self analysis back then, and I was thinking that I'm not such a bad fella, yet in my relationships with women, I'm a total failure. Why is that?"

"You mean committed relationships!"

"What's the difference?"

"David, don't be silly, you know that you are irresponsible, a risk taker, someone who lives by his wits, someone who will move on if the grass is greener. And that's the attraction that you have to someone like me, at this stage of my life. But I don't see beyond that".

"Are you sure that you're just a lawyer?"

"Just a girl tryin' to make a livin'".

"I'm glad I asked you along".

"I'm lovin' every minute, so far. But let's quit all this serious talk. We need to party!"

Melanie was right; I needed to lighten up, to quit trying to find solutions to my personal problems, to stop trying to appease my guilt.

Right on cue, Sandy brought another bottle of champagne.

I suppose that I had been trying to understand what it was that Melanie expected from me from the very first time that we had met and she had become interested in me. Now it had finally penetrated my thick skull; she didn't expect anything from me, she only wanted to have a good time and to enjoy the unparalleled opportunity of being my 'girl friend', for the duration of whatever time we spent together. I understood, but I really couldn't get a handle on her simplistic approach.

Must be a generation thing.

Sandy returned to announce that lunch was being served on the upper deck. We were both surprised, but welcomed the announcement, I know that I was starving, for it had been a long day for me, yet it was only noon. As we made our way to the upper deck, I encountered Mr. Bosko gazing into the water, he looked a little melancholy, as if he had a heavy heart.

"Please come and join us?" I invited.

"Are you sure?"

"Certainly, you look as though you could use a drink".

He followed us on our way upwards. I could smell the aroma of a charcoal grill, and wondered what the crew was preparing.

"Someone told me that the two happiest times in a man's life, are the day that he buys his first boat, and the day that he sells it" I told Mr. Bosko.

"I'm not sure that I agree" he said sadly, "this one is special to me. I've had a great many wonderful experiences on her".

He paused for a moment as he considered his next question. "Will you be retaining the crew? They are extremely competent and they happen to be good friends, that's a rarity among yacht people".

"Yes" I answered "I'm hoping that they will want to stay".

"Do you have any immediate plans for her?"

"We'll be leaving in the morning".

"Really, so soon? And to where?"

"I want to take her back to Ft. Lauderdale to have the Naiads resized before I take an extended cruise".

"That's something I had always planned on, but just never got around to it".

"Can I ask you who the boat is named after?"

He paused before answering, I'm sure he was figuring out how much of the story he would share with two strangers.

"It was named in honour of Princess Diana".

Melanie's female intuition detected something in his speech that led her to ask him if he had actually known her.

"Yes" he answered softly "I met her many years ago in Europe, obviously we were not friends, I wasn't in her social league, but we were both involved in the same charitable endeavors. We met occasionally at fund raising dinners, and became acquainted with one another. Over the course of a few years we continually bumped into each other, almost as if the encounters had been prearranged, it became a bit of a family joke for me. My friends started to refer to her as my Princess. She was the most humble person that I've ever known, there were no airs and graces with her, there was nothing she wouldn't do if the cause was right and there was nowhere that she wouldn't go, no matter the danger to herself, or of the advice given to her by her devoted staff."

"You must have been devastated by her death".

"I've never gotten over it. Such a tragic waste".

"Do you believe that it was an accident?"

"It really doesn't matter what I think. The result is the same" he said bitterly.

He remained deep in thought, almost as if he was reliving his involvement with this woman that he so obviously idolized. We didn't know what to say to break his mood.

Sandy changed it for us, by informing us that lunch was ready.

"We have grilled Mahimahi, plain or Teriyaki, grilled chicken breast with Tarragon, or Hamburgers" she announced, "but first, what can I get everybody to drink?"

Mr. Bosko requested a diet Coke, Melanie chose a glass of wine while I settled on a cold beer. The food smelled and looked very appetizing, everything had been tastefully prepared, the napkins each had a 'Princess' monogram embroidered in their top corners, and the plates, cups and silverware all featured the same logo, even the uniformed crew displayed the word 'Princess' in small gold letters above their white shirt pockets.

The Captain joined us and asked me if everything was satisfactory. I asked him if he would like to have lunch with us, and much to my surprise, he gratefully accepted the invitation. I saw him glance sideways in the direction of Bosko; I assumed that he had never been invited to join the owner for lunch on his previous trips. Melanie discovered that he was from Australia, that his name was Jeremy and 'no' he didn't have a girl friend, nor had he ever been married. He had been a Captain for 11 years and had traveled all around the world; he also convinced Melanie that the 'Princess' was his favorite vessel. I told her later that he would have been foolish to say anything to the contrary.

I had decided not to enlighten the crew of my intention to send the yacht to Bermuda, until Bosko had departed. He would remember that I had made a point of telling him that she was heading to Florida. The fewer people that new of my plans the safer I would be. Melanie had questioned me about my response to Bosko, regarding the future plans for the yacht; she too had been surprised to hear me say that she was going to Florida.

"I'm just being cautious" I told her.

Over lunch Bosko loosened up a little, it must have been the effects of the diet coke, and he entertained us by recounted many stories of his early years in the Bahamas. He had arrived in the Bahamas from Turkey shortly after World War Two, after traveling with his parents through Europe to England and then on to the Bahamas. His father had been a skilled cabinet maker in Turkey, and he had opened a cabinet making enterprise in Nassau in 1948. It was only natural that the son follow in the father's footsteps, so it was that he also learned the skills required in making fine furniture and cabinets. The business flourished, he explained that the Bahamas was in the midst of a building boom and that there was shortage of skilled craftsmen; by 1956 they had 20 employees and had expanded into building complete homes.

"It was a natural evolution for me to take over from my father" Bosko continued "I married a Turkish girl, and brought her here to the Bahamas. We have three sons and two daughters who are all married now and I have a total of six grandchildren. My sons manage the business now; they have built shopping centers, hotels, and marinas. We operate a ready-mix concrete plant, a

87

sewer pipe plant and a water filtration facility. If only our customers would pay their bills, I'd be a rich man"

"You must be very proud of your achievements and your family" commented Melanie.

"I am or course" he replied, "but we fight and argue all the time, often I go for weeks without speaking to one or other of my sons. We're a stubborn group".

"And now you're retired?" I asked.

He laughed at my rhetorical question, "retired! I don't think so. I 'm still the first one in the office every morning".

"It's a habit, I'm sure that your sons would like you to stay away".

"Probably, but I need to do something".

"So play golf or write a book" I suggested, with a smirk.

Bosko laughed "Its too late for any of those, my only recreation is boating, I do enjoy traveling".

"I'm sorry, but I just can't feel sorry for you".

"No" he concluded, "I've had an interesting life, and its so nice to meet a young successful couple like you two, I hope you continue to revel in each others company; take it from it from an old man, but one who knows, the right partner in life is the most important basic element needed for a rewarding life. Not money, or fame, you've got to be with the one you love".

His well intentioned fatherly advice was beginning to make me feel uncomfortable. I changed the direction of the conversation by saying,

"I think I'll have another beer".
"And more wine for me" added Melanie.

It was two o'clock when we reached the dock at the Nassau Harbour Club. I was concerned that there might be an unwelcome reception committee waiting to arrest me, but with a quick scan of the marina, my fears were dispelled. There was no sign of any police activity.

While Bosko was removing his personal effects from the yacht, I went to have a discussion with the Captain. I had decided that the correct protocol was to inform the captain of my plans for the boat, and leave it to him, to relay the information to the other crew members. He was alone on the bridge securing the navigation tools, charts, binoculars and the other equipment that he had used during the trip to Nassau, when I approached him.

"Do you have a moment?" I asked, "we need to talk".

"Of course, sir," he responded.

"I want you to be aware of the immediate plans that I have for the yacht. It's my hope that you and the other members of the crew will stay for a while, because I need to have the vessel delivered to Bermuda as soon as possible. She is to tie up at the Royal Hamilton Yacht Club and to be made ready for a trip to Europe".

"When would you expect to leave?" he asked.

"Tomorrow" I answered, "but I won't be making the trip with you. I'll call you in Bermuda in a few days. My best guess is that you'll be there for at least two weeks before leaving for Europe, so you are all welcome to take a short vacation during that time".

"Thank you, that's very kind of you, I'll inform the crew, and start preparing for an early departure tomorrow".

"Good, we'll be off to the airport in the morning; we have an early flight, so we'll be out of your hair by seven. Here's a telephone number where you can always reach me in an emergency, otherwise you can reach me at the Riviera Hotel in Las Vegas".

"I hope you win a lot of money" he joked.

"I'm not going there to gamble" I replied "at least not in the casinos".

"I've always wanted to go there. I've heard so much about the place".

"In my opinion" I commented "it's one of the worst places on the North American continent; if you made a list of all the aggravating traits of the American people, you'd find most of them in abundance in Las Vegas".

"It's not your favorite place, then?"

"How did you guess?" I laughed, "but I have to go there".

"Well, have a safe trip".

I shook Jeremy's hand and wished him 'bon voyage'.

CHAPTER SIX

I searched for a public telephone away from the throngs of busy airport travelers that were all scurrying about like ants after someone had kicked over their nest. I needed to call Charlie, and a public phone seemed to be the safest choice. I was probably being a little paranoid, but as the actress said to the bishop 'it's better to be safe than sorry'.

It was after 11 o'clock on Friday morning, and I was sure that by now all hell had broken loose in Spanish Wells, with the discovery of the bank robbery. He answered on the third ring.

"Charlie?"

"Where are you?" he asked.

"Miami airport. What's happening?"

"Absolutely nothing. I was at the Royal Bank in Harbour Island just an hour ago. Of course I didn't ask any questions, but there was no hint of a problem and no rumors. You can bet that the whole place would have been buzzing if they'd known".

"They must have decided to keep it quiet for some reason".

Charlie suggested that the Bank didn't want to be embarrassed by having to confess that their security was lax, or that they were a day or two late in making the discovery.

"The plane landed in Fort Lauderdale with the fish. Nobody asked any questions. The pilot is on his way back now".

"It's baffling" I pondered, "do you think that maybe they suspect someone local, and that they are hoping that if they wait the thief will return the money?"

"You can bet that the Royal Bank is not going to sit still for a robbery of this magnitude. But I don't understand their policy".

"There was no problem at the airport when we left Nassau" I told him.

"We?" he asked, "whose we?"

"I brought my attorney along" I laughed.

"David? Will you never learn?"

"I am learning" I challenged, "from you!"

"Can I ask you where you're traveling to? I assume that you didn't go to the airport to watch the planes depart".

"Vegas, for a few days".

"Don't gamble away all the money!"

"Not a chance, it's on the way to Bermuda".

Charlie was silent for a moment.

"Bermuda? Why Bermuda? How's it getting there?" he asked.

I knew that eventually I would tell Charlie how I had converted the Bahamian dollars into a luxury yacht, but now was not the time. The less he knew the better, at least until I had completed the final part of my plan. I knew that I could trust Charlie, but he did have a tendency to brag sometimes, and I could just hear him bragging to someone he wanted to impress by hinting to them that he knew something about the bank robbery. It would only take one word to the wrong person.

"By special delivery, and that's all I'm saying".

I waited while he digested all the information; he was like a big fish taking my bait.

"Where are you staying in Vegas?" he asked innocently.

"The Riviera"

"There's a convention scheduled there, I think".

"Yes, there is. The International Trading Convention".

"I'm a member, have been for years" he stated.

"Me too" I told him.

"Is that's why you're going there? What's going on David? How would you feel about me joining you there?"

"It's a free country" I smiled as he swallowed the bait "You know I enjoy your company".

He continued to make his plans for a visit to Vegas using me as his sounding board, as if he needed my approval. He finally agreed to meet us in two days time, but he was still undecided whether or not he would travel alone. If I was a betting man, I would say the odds of him arriving unaccompanied would be five to one against.

I had completed the next part of my plan; Charlie would meet us in Vegas. I might need his expertise.

Melanie was waiting in the coffee shop while I was making my calls; we had two hours to kill before the flight was scheduled to leave. I found her catching a nap at the table.

She heard me as I pulled out a chair to join her.

"You were a long time" she said. "is everything ok?"

"Fine. Charlie's going to meet us in Las Vegas".

She looked disappointed at the news.

"I was hoping to have you all to myself" she purred.

"He'll have his own room" I laughed. "I might need an ally. Anymore nights like last night and I'll be worn out".

"I had a wonderful time, and I thought you did too?"

Last night had been a night to remember. Melanie must have decided that my last night in the Bahamas was to be one that I would never forget. I could blame it on the champagne, but that would not be totally true, it was more of a feeling of triumph for me and I would guess one of unmitigated pleasure for Melanie. The very fact that we were together on a fabulous yacht, in a tropical location, being waited on by a conscientious crew, must have contributed to our euphoric feelings.

After finishing another bottle of champagne in our stateroom, Melanie had decided that we should shower together. She had discovered that the shower stall had five shower heads, located at different levels and in very strategic positions. She turned them on full, sprayed some perfume into the streams of water, turned to me with a childish grin on her damp face and slowly disrobed. I followed suit, but I'm sure that my performance was not as seductive as hers. She was as playful as a kitten, a kitten in heat that is. There were no parts of either one of us that were not explored, washed, rinsed, kissed or caressed, it was wonderfully sensual, stimulating, but mostly fun.

If I am typical of most men, then I can say that our relationship reached not only a different level, but for me a much more relaxed level. I have always had the notion that in the early days of any relationship, the man, the natural aggressor is at a disadvantage. My reasoning is simple, he expects more, he wants more, he's impatient, and he's uncomfortable until he successfully satisfies his mate. He's unable to separate his feelings of tenderness, love, and consideration from his natural sexual urgings. Only after his sexual appetite is appeased is he able to become tuned in to his partners needs, and become comfortable, without being continually aroused. Some women may interpret this as a macho put down, when really the reverse is true. It's only after that first sexual experience that some men learn to appreciate their partners for who they are, and not what they are. With Melanie this is exactly what happened, that first sexual experience was out of the way and now I could get beyond my sexual urge and delight in the experience of knowing her, and be comfortable frolicking with her in a totally relaxed manner.

The Paradise Island Harbour Club met and exceeded our expectations. The Club is situated on the Eastern end of Paradise Island and its open- air nautical bar and restaurant are both charming and tastefully decorated. We were shown to a candle lit table that provided us with an exquisite view across the harbour from the twinkling lights of the Nassau Yacht Club and the distant shore of Nassau's eastern outskirts. A three piece ensemble was playing quiet romantic music in the background and I knew that it could lead to only one thing. But I relished in the thought 'cause now I was comfortable.

The food was without equal, the wine was magnificent, the service impeccable and the company was unmatched. Melanie had outdone herself; as she had entered every eye had focused on her, the men were noticeably silent while their wives had glared at her with envy. The evening had flashed by, neither of us aware of the time, nor of the other patrons in the restaurant. We had danced with a flare to the lively Island beat and when the music slowed we had moulded our bodies together and became one, as we floated across the dance floor. It had been pure magic.

Our flight was being called, so we gathered our carry-on bags and prepared to board. Melanie had been uncharacteristically quiet during our wait in the lounge, like me, she had been reliving the events of the previous day. But unlike me her thoughts were focused on the evening's activities, whereas mine had been concentrated on the early morning shenanigans. From the smile on her face, it was easy to guess that she was remembering the boat ride back to the 'Princess', the red rose that I had placed on her pillow before we had left for dinner, the gentle massage that I given her before we had made love and the sheer ecstasy of our passionate consummation. She sighed audibly as she recalled each memorable moment.

"A penny for your thoughts".

"They're worth much more than a penny" she smiled "they're priceless. I'm on cloud nine".

I looked out of the window to check the clouds "I don't see any numbers on them".

"They're only visible to a select few, and I'm sorry to say that you're obviously not one of them. It's a girl thing".

She tucked her arm under mine and leaned her head onto my shoulder. I closed my eyes, but I couldn't sleep, my mind was racing out of control as I tried to prepare myself for the next few days. I knew that it was important to complete my business in Vegas as quickly as possible. My plan was to trade the 'Princess' for diamonds, then sell the diamonds and deposit the money in my Swiss bank account. Only when the money was in my account would I consider the mission completed.

The convention that was to take place in Vegas was the largest of its kind in the world and would be attended by a truly international clientele, with members coming from every corner of the world.

The International Association of Traders was an organization that had been formed more than forty years ago. I had been a member for twelve years, and over the years I had formed many close alliances with a diverse group of professional traders. Trading and bartering has become a huge business and each year it expands into more and more countries where taxation and Government controls continue to impede capitalistic growth. At this convention it would be possible to trade for practically any product or service known anywhere in the world.

I was in a dilemma regarding my involvement with Melanie, should I come clean and tell her about the source of the money that had been used to purchase 'Princess', or should I continue to let her think that Charlie had been the purchaser?. A part of me wanted to be honest with her, no matter what the consequences, after all a relationship based on an untruth could only spiral downwards, yet there was another part that of me that subscribed to the old adage, that what you didn't know wouldn't hurt you. Melanie was no fool, she would smell a rat as soon as she reunited with Charlie, she had already hinted to me that she was having trouble understanding the exact reason for the trip to Vegas, and I was pretty sure that when she discovered that the yacht was to be traded away she would ask me some penetrating and embarrassing questions. There were two choices, either she had to know, or the relationship needed to be terminated.

Maybe Charlie had been correct when he had chided me for bringing Melanie along, was I guilty of thinking with my little head instead of the big thicker one?

I made my decision and gently prodded Melanie to wake her; I made it seem like an accident, apologizing profusely for interrupting her sleep.

"What's wrong?" she asked groggily.

"I'm sorry; I didn't mean to wake you"

"How long have I been asleep?"

"Just an hour or so. I missed you".

She snuggled against my shoulder and closed her eyes once again.

"Melanie" I whispered "I need to talk to you".

She was awake in a second "Is something wrong?"

"No, nothing's wrong" I assured her.

"Are you gonna talk dirty to me?" she said seductively.

"No, this serious".

"You're too serious", she stated, "you've been awake all this time thinking about me and you've decided to leave your wife and ask me to marry you!"

"You're right" I admitted "how did you guess?"

"David, don't tease me. What do you really want to tell me?"

"Just that I'm falling for you, and I hope that what I am about to confess to won't change anything between us".

"This is serious" she commented.

There was no easy way to tell her that I was a thief and a scoundrel, so I plunged right in "The cash that I used to buy the 'Princess' did not come from Charlie, as you surmised. It came from the Royal Bank in Spanish Wells. I stole it!"

She didn't bat an eye, so I forged ahead. "I've sent the yacht to Bermuda, and we're going to Las Vegas to meet with someone who will trade precious stones for the yacht. It has nothing to do with Charlie. It was all my doing".

"Wow, David that's quite a confession" she said, "now I have a confession of my own. You already know that I'm lawyer, but what you don't know, is that I'm also an undercover agent for the Bank".

She reached over and grabbed me by the ear.

"You're under arrest" she stated.

Then she laughed, "I scared you didn't I?"

For a moment I thought that she was telling the truth and that her performance of the past few days had been nothing more than a convincing act. But her laugh had given her away and I laughed with her, with considerable relief.

"Yes you did" I admitted, "you really got to me. But you don't seem to be upset by my deceit?"

"I told you from the very beginning that I was just along for the ride, and so far I'm enjoying every minute. Yes, I was curious when I saw all that cash and I've known for some time that you were harbouring secrets from me, but that's fine. I knew that you'd tell me when you thought I needed to know".

"And now's the time" I interjected "the robbery was a piece of cake, because the bank knew that a large amount of Bahamian dollars would be virtually impossible to exchange for a negotiable currency, they hardly bothered with any security."

"And you've found a way to spend the money, by purchasing a valuable asset from a Bahamian, who by law is restricted from having foreign currency. That was pretty smart of you!"

"But it doesn't end there" I said, "a yacht like the 'Princess' is traceable, and difficult to sell. If it returned to the United States, even though it was built there, it would be subject to import duty because it had been exported and had been foreign registered. The paper trail that a vessel of its size generates could lead to an investigation by the Coast Guard or the Maritime Authority of just about any country".

"So you're trading her for a bunch of baubles?"

"Hardly baubles. Diamonds yes, and plenty of them. I know quite a lot about diamonds, having seen more than my share from both sides of the fence. You'll learn a lot about trading and diamonds in the next few days, it should be a very profitable exercise for us both".

"Can I keep one or two?"

"Why is it that women the world over are fascinated by diamonds?" I asked, "they're only pieces of carbon made to look pretty, yet I've never met a member of the opposite sex that doesn't go gaga at the mention of diamonds".

"We're programmed at an early age".

"You are closer to the truth than you may have imagined. The marketing of diamonds is probably the most successful venture in the world. 'A diamond is forever' has become more than just a catchy slogan, for every girl it has become the recognizable sign of commitment from their potential marriage partner, and the poor guy is faced with having to spend his hard earned money to buy her a diamond. And the bigger the better, and even though he can't afford it he knows that he's required to show his devotion with the purchase of a 'rock'. It's the only major purchase that most couples make, where neither one of them has a clue about value or worth, except for a brief directive from a TV expert; they place their trust in the reputation of the jeweler, and hope for the best. Can you imagine buying a car the same way?"

"But surely they are a good investment" suggested Melanie.

"You're kidding! They are a poor investment. Just try selling your five thousand dollar engagement ring to a jewelry store, you'll be lucky to get a thousand for it".

"How many diamonds do you expect to receive for the 'Princess'?"

"The secret of successful trading rather than selling is to find merchandise for which a true value is difficult to establish. The yacht is a good example, we know that I paid eight million, but it has been highly customized, exquisitely furnished and loaded with expensive electronic equipment, making it hard to valuate. There is no 'book' value, only an insurance appraisal, which is normally very high. It would be difficult to trade a standard Ford Explorer for example, the value is easy to verify, no one will trade for more than its book value. For trading purposes I'll value the 'Princess' at twenty five million, and try to trade her for close to a hundred million in diamonds".

"You're talking about dollars like grains of sand, I can't believe it".

"A hundred million in diamonds is only worth about ten percent of that amount, in other words ten to twelve million, close to the actual value of the yacht. All the values are highly inflated, but the professionals know that, and can usually trade or barter at the correct numbers".

"You appear to have everything planned, but let me ask you, how will you sell the diamonds? And to who? And if you can sell them, why wouldn't the person you hope to buy them from, sell them himself instead of trading for a yacht?"

"I have an ace up my sleeve that only a few people are aware of. I'll tell you what it is sometime soon, but for now we should forget about diamonds", I suggested "in fact, I could use a cold drink or a cup of tea. How about you?"

"Tea for two sounds nice".

The pilot made an announcement that off to the right hand side of the plane we would be able to see the Grand Canyon. It proved to be another exciting episode for Melanie as she scrambled around the plane trying to find the best vantage point.

"One day I'll be taking a rafting trip through that Canyon" she said "I saw a short film about such a trip and it was breathtaking, since then I've always wanted to go".

"If only I'd known, I would have arranged it for you".

"So what have you arranged?"

"You now that I hate Las Vegas, so my idea is to spend as little time there as possible. There are a couple of places worth visiting that are within driving distance, I thought we might pack a picnic lunch and take a look".

"You really mean it? I had visions of me being left alone while you were busy making these big deals in a smoke filled room somewhere".

"The 'big deal' won't take long to complete once I've found the right contact. I'll have lots of time to spend with my favorite lawyer".

"So tell me where we are going?"

"The Hoover Dam and Zion National Park".

"I had no idea that Hoover Dam was close by".

"About 30 miles away, we'll take a helicopter ride. You'll love it!"

"I've never flown in a helicopter. How exciting".

"It's the only way to go".

"I can hardly wait, and where is the Zion place?"

"In Utah, three hours by car. I thought that we would hike along one of the many trails, explore a cave or two, then find a quiet spot for a picnic".

"You certainly know how to show a girl a good time" she sighed "how can I possibly pay you back?"

"I'm sure you'll find a way".

The mini suite that I had reserved at the Riviera was far from mini, I was tempted to ask how large were the regular ones, but the bell hop hardly understood English, so any attempt at a joke would have been wasted on him.

"This is larger than my whole apartment" Melanie said, as she danced around the room. She kicked off her shoes and jumped up and down on one of the beds "which one shall we sleep in?"

"I didn't bring you all this way to sleep" I growled "you can sleep when you get home!"

"Oh David, I'm frightened, are you gonna ravish me?" she mocked.

"Haven't you ever been ravished before?" I asked in a threatening voice.

"I don't think so, but I'm sure you'll be a gentle ravisher. So when do you start?"

I unbuttoned my shirt and threw it onto the floor as I approached the king size bed where Melanie was cowering in fear, she tried to suppress her giggles as she anticipated my next move.

"Get undressed" I ordered.

"But I'm so young and innocent" she cried "I'm only thirteen".

"Dam, lucky I'm not superstitious then!" I yelled.

By now I had shed my pants; I reached across the bed to where she was attempting to find a measure of safety by huddling close to the headboard.

"Come here, Deary. See what I've brought you".

"Is it a present?" she asked.

"Yes. Look!"

"But it doesn't have a bow on it" she laughed.

I couldn't keep up the pretense any longer, I laughed along with her, and then I ravished her, or maybe she ravished me. I'm not sure which.

One of the few redeeming features of Las Vegas is that they do attract some of the world's best entertainers, and after studying the list of personalities that were performing in the many hotels around town, I found to my surprise that my namesake David Sanborn was appearing in the lounge downstairs.

Melanie had been watching me as I had searched through the complimentary magazine that had been placed on the coffee table, she noticed my change of expression "You look as though you've found a long lost friend" she commented.

"Hardly" I replied, "but one of my favorite jazz musicians is playing here".

"Right here? In the hotel?"

"Yes, in the lounge".

"Well, let's go!"

The song 'Since I fell for you' that was featured on an album named 'Double Vision' played beautifully by Bob James on keyboard and David Sanborn on alto sax, had become one of my all time favorites. It had been recorded in 1986 with a relatively unknown vocalist, whose interpretation of the words and music earned him a Grammy nomination. The vocalist was Al Jarreau who is now recognized as one of the great male jazz singers of our time. On occasion I had been known to give my rendition of the song. There are some songs that you never ever forget, this was one of them, but to date my version had been limited to the shower.

There was plenty of room in the lounge; Mr. Sanborn was not a household name to the clientele that frequented the Riviera, to me that was a plus but I'm sure that the management felt otherwise. In my college years I had played tenor saxophone in a London based jazz group and I was quite good for an amateur. I had been very fortunate to 'sit in' with many visiting artists and the biggest thrill of my brief musical life had been the night that Stan Getz had visited the club and joined me on stage; he was then and still is my idol.

Listening to the improvisations of the artists on the small stage in the lounge transported me back to my beginnings as a musician. To the hours of practice and rehearsal that I had endured and to the frustration of not being good enough to play the difficult passages that these professionals breezed through.

"I need to go to the ladies room" announced Melanie just as we were seated.

"Just wait a minute, will you? We've hardly been here for any length of time. D'you know that I'd have given my right arm to have played like that" I said dreamily as I listened to Sanborn's sax.

"You couldn't have played at all with one arm" stated Melanie.

"Very funny" I said sarcastically, "it was a dream of mine to be able to play like that. It's strange the way life twists and turns, having dreams and making plans has never worked for me".

"Am I supposed to feel sorry for you?"

"No, I was just making conversation. I doubt if you'd want to hear the sad, heart wrenching saga of my life as a struggling musician".

"I only brought one box of tissues, it'll have to wait for another time".

"You have no compassion, no feelings in that cold heart of yours" I said loudly, so that the customers at the adjoining table could hear.

"That's right" Melanie shouted "I got problems of my own; I don't have to listen to your whimpering".

Playing her role to perfection she pushed her chair away from the table so hard, that it fell backwards, and then she stalked out of the room.

"You bitch" I yelled after her.

There was a momentary hush in the lounge as everyone watched her leave. I remained at our table, ordered another drink and listened to the cool music.

She was back in ten minutes. She settled into her chair, put her arms around me and kissed me hard on the mouth for thirty seconds.

Someone actually booed.

A trip to Las Vegas would not be complete without at least one night of gambling. I was surprised to learn that Melanie had never been to a casino, those in the Bahamas being off limits to Bahamians. She was eager to get started, so being the nice guy that I am, I handed her two hundred dollars and told her to pay me back from her winnings. I left her feeding money into a slot machine and went to find a seat at one of the black jack tables.

Gambling is meant to be fun, most people will tell you about the great time they had gambling in Las Vegas; this is after they're home. A survey of the tonight's customers, and in my experience every night's customers, confirmed for me the reality that no one is enjoying themselves, with the exception of those that partake in craps. The long faces on the group seated around my table playing blackjack were typical of all the gamblers from anywhere in the world, they were sullen, miserable and downright rude if the occasion arose.

At least two out of the eight people at the table had enough chips to choke a horse sitting in neat piles in front of them, and I don't think that they started out with that many. I squeezed into my seat between two ugly people from a bus tour; I'm not sure which was worse, the smell of the cheap perfume or the smell of the cheaper cigar. It was if we were all enemies, all trying to win the same limited amount of money from the casino, someone should tell them that there was enough for everyone. There were no greetings, no smiles, no introductions and no gestures of good luck, if anything they resented the interruption to the game that each new player brought. I knew better than to exhibit my natural charm and wit, it would have been wasted on this miserable group. Maybe they're all counting cards, I thought, and concentrating hard, but a quick look around and it was obvious that most of these morons couldn't count higher than twenty, that being the total sum of their digits. Well maybe twenty one for the men. A thought struck me; maybe that's where the name of the game came from.

Boring is the only way to describe this game, my winning streak did nothing to relieve the boredom; it just made it more difficult to walk away. I could hear cheers of encouragement coming from the far end of the room, and I surmised that a group of happy drunks were enjoying the thrill of winning at craps. I was tempted to join them, but the rules of the game, and the lingo used are different to those commonly used in Europe, I didn't need to be singled out as being different. I collected my chips from the blackjack table and wandered slowly in the direction of the noisy crowd. They were not playing craps, they were lined up ten deep behind one of the dollar slot machines urging the lone gambler to keep on winning. As the bells rang signaling yet another big win, the cheers increased in volume, these folks were having a good time watching someone else win. It was like a conspiracy against the house, as long as someone won, they all felt better. I craned my neck to catch a glimpse of the lucky winner with the hot hand. It was Melanie.

Not wanting to interfere while she was the center of attraction, I made my way back to the lounge in the hope of catching the last set. The crowd in the lounge had grown and there were no empty tables available, so I found a seat at the bar and ordered a drink. I was pleased to see that a girl vocalist had joined the group. This addition gave a new dimension to the music and provided David Sanborn with the opportunity to display his improvisational ability by weaving a lyrical obbligato around the melody. A customer requested 'Since I fell for You' before I had had a chance to. I matched the girl singer word for word, phrase for phrase from my seat at the bar. I should have known better. Still with the microphone in her hand she left the stage and walked the few short steps to the bar, the crowd urged her on as they anticipated her next move. She took my hand and led me up onto the stage, the familiar saxophone intro was repeated and we sang together just as if we had rehearsed together. In the second chorus I even attempted to emulate Al Jarreau, a few knowledgeable customers appreciated my tribute to the great singer and as we reached the final climatic crescendo, the patrons stood and gave us a standing ovation.

After some congratulatory words from the band members, I left the stage and returned to my seat at the bar. Everyone wanted to shake my hand, or buy me a drink, and I was affectionately slapped on the back by all those in close proximity, as I squeezed my way through the standing room only crowd.

"Can I have your autograph?" a familiar voice asked.

"Hi there. Did you win all their money?"

"Not quite, but I had fun and did Ok. You were sensational up there, I heard the singing and came to see what was going on, I could hardly believe my eyes when I found out that it was you. You continue to amaze me David. Is there anything that you can't do?"

I thought for a moment before answering.

"Skate backwards; play the violin; keep a secret; be faithful! There're plenty more but those came to mind. Now tell me how much you won?"

She made sure that no one could hear her as she whispered in my ear "Three thousand two hundred dollars. Here's your two hundred".

She pushed two hundred dollars into my hand. I was so excited for her; she was glowing with pride as she hugged me.

"I had so much fun, I couldn't lose, the money just kept coming, the bells kept ringing and the crowd got louder and louder. I can't wait for tomorrow".

I was more thrilled with the three thousand that Melanie had won than I was for the eight million that I'd stolen just two days ago.

"Shall I cancel the trip to the Dam, and the picnic, so you can gamble all day tomorrow?" I asked.

"That's a tough choice"

"You might win a fortune".

"But I might lose too. No, we'll go to the Dam".

"Damn right" I agreed.

CHAPTER SEVEN

Charlie Wolfsen hung up the phone after taking the call from David. He thought about the confession that David had made, boasting about taking his lawyer with him on the trip to Las Vegas. He concluded that he must be out of his mind to take a coloured tramp on such a trip, when he had a beautiful and loving wife waiting for him at home.

Laura had always held a special place in Charlie's heart. From the first time that they had met Charlie had wanted to be with her, but Laura had been swept off her feet by David and all he could do was to stand by and watch their romance blossom. Charlie had never met anybody else that had the same allure as Laura and on those rare occasions when he had dated he always found himself comparing his date to Laura, and none of his dates had come close.

Over the years since her marriage to David, he had kept track of them both, always remembering their wedding anniversaries, their birthdays and checking from time to time on their activities. He maintained his air of indifference to their numerous marital problems, but secretly his animosity towards David grew whenever he learned of a new problem that David had caused. Many times he had gritted his teeth and shuddering with disgust as David had recounted stories of his sexual escapades. Now Charlie would be the first to admit that he was no saint himself, but as he readily told anyone who would listen to him, "I may cheat at cards, and I'll cheat on my taxes every chance I get, but I would never cheat on my wife, if I had one".

Fifteen years had passed since Charlie had seized the opportunity to become involved in pornography. He had dabbled in the movie business for a while but his lack of taste had been reflected in the one or two miserable box office failures that he had produced. But his foot was in the door and when he overheard a group of his movie associates talking about the potential of the new Internet, he had been quick to jump on the band wagon. Internet pornography had become one of the fastest growing evils in society and is a billion dollar industry. Charlie started making X rated five minute expose films, and soon progressed to nastier and viler enterprises. Within five years he was the 'King' of porn with his picture on the cover of Beast magazine and with every pervert, pimp, prostitute and porn star vying for his attention.

He made a fortune and carefully extricated himself from the filth that was his bread and butter. He attempted to elevate himself to a position of respect in the legitimate entertainment industry, but the major portion of his income was still derived from his original pornographic investments.

He expanded his horizons and produced music videos; he opened two upscale night clubs, while he continued to surround himself with trashy women and star struck hopefuls. He used them all without regard for their feelings, to him they were merchandise to be sold or used for a profit.

The fortune he made bought him the trinkets that are commonplace to the rich and famous; fabulous homes in the best and most exclusive parts of the world; dates with super models and movie stars; fast exotic cars and airplanes. But he knew that he didn't fit, and try as he might he could not overcome his desire for his old heart throb, Laura.

Charlie had never been one to miss an opportunity and David's confession had provided him with one that he couldn't pass up. He placed a call to his chief of security.

"Mac?" he asked, "is that you? You're voice sounds different".

"It's me. What can I do for you?"

"I want some pictures taken. Compromising pictures of a stupid buddy of mine, who is cheating on his wife".

"Where is he?"

"Vegas. He's staying at the Riviera with his girl friend".

"Send me the details; a recent picture of him would be nice"

"You'll have them in an hour. When can you leave?"

"I can be there in the morning. Any limitations?"

"None. Do what ever you have to. But be discreet".

"I'll call tomorrow from Vegas. Where will you be?"

"I'm flying to London tonight, call me there".

Charlie felt a need to be close to Laura, not in contact but within call if she should need a 'friend'. With this in mind he closed 'Shangri La' and flew to Miami to connect with a British Airways flight to London.

Charlie maintained an apartment in the West End of London and a home on Millionaires Row in the suburb of Mill Hill. The apartment afforded him the luxury of being where the action was and was an inducement to the many women that he used during his stay.

He was confident in his ability to persuade Laura that she was being foolish to continue being humiliated by her unfaithful husband, and pictures of David with his 'nigger' whore would convince her that he was right.

He was Annie's Godfather, but he was troubled by her whenever he was around her. He knew that she hated him, only a teenager was perceptive enough to be able to see through his guise of indifferent friend. He knew that he would have to separate the daughter from her mother if he was to be successful in his conquest.

The moment he arrived at his London apartment after his flight from Miami, he placed a call to Laura.

"Hi Laura, its Charlie. Just back in town for a few days and I wanted to tell you that I ran into David in the Bahamas. He seemed relaxed and well, he had a nice tan and was enjoying the local colour. He gave me a message for you. Call me back when you arrive home, my number is Mayfair six one two six".

Laura's answering machine clicked off as Charlie hung up his phone.

115

Charlie switched on his computer to check to see if there were any email messages. There was one from Mac with an attachment. He read the message, clicked the attachment icon and gazed triumphantly at the dozen pictures of David and his whore. Most were taken in the casino and showed them holding hands, hugging and kissing. A few had been taken in a lounge and again it was plain to see that this was more than a casual Whore/ John affair. David's hands were all over her and she was pretending to enjoy his amorous attention. The quality of the pictures was outstanding, it was clear that Mac was proficient at his job. Charlie reread the brief message from Mac. He expected more pictures would be taken tomorrow with more intimate details. Charlie decided not to wait, the pictures he had were incriminating enough to cause Laura to consider ending her marriage, and if more pictures arrived so much the better.

Laura returned Charlie's call later the same day. He explained that he had met David in Harbour Island and that they had had dinner together. When she asked about David's message, Charlie would only say that he needed to see her in person and suggested that they meet for a drink somewhere. He didn't want to go to Laura's home for fear of encountering Annie.

A 'date' was arranged for the next evening. Laura would be in the City she explained and could meet Charlie by six. Charlie suggested the bar at the Savoy, a place that was well known and not the type of locale that would suggest that their meeting was anything but a casual re-acquaintance between two old friends. If he had suggested his club her guard would have been up and his intentions hard to explain.

"Who was on the phone?" asked Annie.

"It was Charlie. He met up with Dad in the Bahamas, he has a message for me" Laura replied.

"What's the message?"

"He didn't say. I'm meeting him tomorrow evening for a drink. He'll tell me then".

"Why wouldn't he tell you on the phone?"

"I dunno. He said that he wanted to tell me in person. Why are you acting so suspiciously?"

"It just sounds weird to me, that's all".

"I'm sure it's nothing important. If it had been, Dad would have called. So you'll be on your own tomorrow evening; I won't be home 'til late".

"Late? Why? You're only meeting for a drink?"

"I'm sure Charlie will want to take me to dinner".

"Mum, he's a creep. I can't stand him".

"He's not so bad. And he's rich and single".

"And Dad's friend remember" Annie interjected.

"I've known him just as long as your father has; in fact we met on the same day. He's always had a crush on me!"

"Mum! Please!"

"It's true. I've always known, but he's never even made a pass".

The next morning Laura took a little extra time dressing and preening herself. She wore her sexiest business suit, high heels and more make up than on her normal days. She knew it was only Charlie, but she was going on a 'date' and that in itself was a good enough reason to spruce herself up. Annie had noticed the change in her mother's appearance and had whistled at her as she had watched her enter her car and show a length of her shapely legs.

Charlie was waiting in the lobby as Laura entered the Savoy Hotel. They hugged briefly and exchanged smiles as Charlie took her arm and escorted her into the bar. They found a table and ordered a drink.

"You look wonderful Laura. You never look a day older. How do you do it?"

"Thank you. I feel older. You look tanned Charlie" she said.

"I have a house in the Bahamas. I just arrived from there yesterday. It's where I met David. How come you weren't with him?" he asked.

"I couldn't get away, just too busy".

Charlie reached into his pocket and extracted an envelope of photographs. He showed them to Laura as he said, "This is my house on the beach, it's called 'Shangri-La'. There's David drinking by the pool".

"It looks fabulous Charlie. Who are all the girls?"

"Most of them work for me, commercials, movies, videos, you know. A trip to the Bahamas is a perk for them".

Laura leafed through the pile of pictures, examining each one carefully. She selected two from the stack and pointed to a picture of Melanie with her husband, "Who's she?" she asked.

"A local hooker, I think. She came with David!"

"What do you mean, she came with David?"

"I met them at Coral Sands, they were having lunch together. I asked David to join me at my house for a cook out, and he dragged her along".

"And you think that she's a hooker?"

"Laura, look at her. I was embarrassed to have her at my pool, with my friends".

"The bastard. The dirty son of a bitch". Laura cursed, "and black. I'll never forgive him"

Laura continued to look at the pictures as she fought back her tears. Charlie reached into his pocket and extracted the pictures that had been sent from Vegas. He placed them on the table in front of Laura.

"You need to look at these" he said.

Laura flipped through the new pictures.

"Where is this?"

"Las Vegas" Charlie replied, "he took her there for a good time. In fact they're still there".

"I just can't believe this. Oh I've had my suspicions, and I could've overlooked a casual fling perhaps, but to actually take a nigger whore on a trip to Vegas is beyond belief. It's over Charlie. This time he's gone too far. I'll sue the bastard for all he's got. How could he do this to me? And more importantly, to Annie!"

Charlie moved his chair around the table to be close to Laura. He hugged her and felt her tremble as she cried into his shoulder.

"I feel like a heel betraying my friend, but I couldn't stand by and see him hurt you. I had to tell you what was going on. But this is hard for me because I love you both".

"It's Ok Charlie, I'm glad you've shown me what a bastard he is. When he comes back, I'll kick him out. He can have his whore!"

Slowly during the course of the evening and fortified with a continual supply of drinks courtesy of Charlie, Laura slowly regained control of her emotions and began to make rational plans for her immediate future.

CHAPTER EIGHT

Rudy's helicopter tours advertised a complete package tour of the Hoover Dam and its surroundings, which included a free pick-up from the hotel, and for an additional fee they would fly into the Grand Canyon, land on the canyon floor at the Hualapai Indian Reservation, where it was possible to hire a guide for a day of white water rafting. I made the necessary arrangements by telephone without telling Melanie, as far as she understood we were only making a one hour trip to the Hoover Dam.

The sight- seeing helicopter held a total of six passengers, each person had a window seat for an unimpeded view, and the seats could be swiveled or locked in position but best of all the interior was air conditioned. We lifted off from the heliport, climbed to a height of about five hundred feet and followed the highway below us to the Dam.

Melanie was like a kid in a toy shop, each time the pilot changed direction, she shrieked with delight as a new vista came into sight. As we came closer to the Dam the helicopter slowed and descended, giving us all an incredible panoramic view of this man made wonder.

Suddenly the ground below us disappeared as we flew over the canyon, it felt as if we had dropped several hundred feet when in reality we were still flying level. This produced the loudest of her squeals from Melanie but was followed closely by those of the two other ladies on board.

"This is so beautiful" she declared to everyone.

The helicopter had now descended to within a hundred feet of the surface of Lake Mead and had turned south west. We could see the top of the Dam directly ahead and as we flew over it, its immense proportions boggled all of our collective minds, the thickness of the wall of concrete that held back the river was as wide as a city street even at the top, and at the bottom it must have been three times this thickness. The pilot provided a running commentary, reciting the statistical information that we should have paid attention to, but it was hard to listen and to observe at the same time. We made another circuit over the lake and back to the Dam, where we hovered for a few minutes allowing the passengers ample time to take plenty of photographs.

"I should have brought a camera" stated Melanie. She gripped my hand across the aisle "This is the most exciting trip I've ever taken".

"We're not done yet" I said.

"What do you mean?"

"I have a surprise in store. Instead of the Zion National Park, we're going rafting on the Colorado river".

"When?"

"Next, this is just the first part of the trip"

As I spoke the pilot climbed back to his operational height, he told everyone to make sure that their seat belts were secure as he directed the chopper back to Lake Mead for the flight to the Grand Canyon.

"I'm speechless" said Melanie, "it's beyond my wildest dream. How did you know that I've always wanted to go white water rafting?"

"You mentioned it on the flight to Vegas".

"I did? I don't remember".

The helicopter circled at the edge of the canyon then slowly descended to a plateau that overlooked the river below.

"We'll take a fifteen minute break here, before we descend to the Canyon floor" the pilot said.

We all disembarked to stretch our legs and breathe in the cool mountain air. I had noticed one passenger in particular sitting in the seat ahead of Melanie, who looked familiar. I pulled her away from the other passengers, as I tried to remember where I had seen him. Then it came to me.

"Do you recognize that man?" I asked as I nodded in the direction of the man in question.

"The one in the suit?" Melanie asked.

"Yes. I recognized him earlier, but couldn't place him. He was one of the crowd that was watching you win at the slot machine yesterday. I saw him in the crowd, and later he was in the lounge, keeping an eye on us".

"Could be a coincidence. Who do you think he is?"

"I've no idea who he is, but there's only one person that he can be working for, and that's Charlie!"

"But Charlie's your friend".

"Sure he is, but Charlie doesn't like not knowing what's going on. I'm sure that this guy has been told to stick close to us. I don't entirely trust Charlie, because he knows that the best people to steal from are thieves. I can't run to the law to report a robbery, so until the money is in the bank in Switzerland I have to be on my guard".

"You honestly believe that Charlie would steal from you?"

"Oh yes, I have no doubts on that score, and he'd enjoy doing it".

The group was ready to re-board for the flight to the canyon floor, Melanie and I joined them and tried to act nonchalant.

The flight through the canyon past Spencer Canyon and the Bowl of Fire was breath taking, and as we slowly descended the four thousand feet to the floor of the Canyon and the Hualapai Indian Reservation, we saw a number of incredible rock formations, some were as red as fire and some had eerie intricate shapes that had been carved out by centuries of erosion.

After landing we were met by three Indians who introduced themselves as a father and his two sons. The father would be the guide on the water, while the two youths were there to make sure that we were all prepared with life jackets, paddles, plastic bags for cameras and valuables, and helmets. The men wore red helmets and the women wore yellow. I don't know why. An eight man raft sat at the waters edge awaiting us. The rafters for the trip were Melanie, the 'spy' in the suit, an older couple, who we later discovered were on their honeymoon, two girls who were probably lesbians, and me.

Running Water, that's what the guide called himself, gave us a quick summation of what we could expect, he assured us that it was very safe but we should follow his instructions at all times and not to be nervous or frightened. He explained that he would steer from the stern; he selected me to be on the port side at the front of the raft and the 'spy' to be on the starboard side. The balance of the crew was positioned in the raft with Melanie at the rear with the guide.

"Be a shame if he got his suit wet" I whispered to Melanie, as I nodded towards the 'spy'.

"You're up to something?"

"Accidents will happen" I laughed.

As part of our preparation we had been given a map of the route that we would follow, it included an elevation sketch to show us the total amount or our descent and the heights of the various rapids we would encounter along the way. The journey would include several class 3 and 4 rapids, and judging from the scale on the map, I estimated that the drop in elevation at each rapid would be between 10 and 15 feet.

I showed Melanie my map with my calculations scribbled in the margin.

"What do think?" I asked.

"Piece of cake" she replied with a scoff.

The 'spy' looked ridiculous with his red helmet on his head and his orange life jacket strapped over his suit, he hadn't even removed his tie and I noticed that his shoes were more suitable for ballroom dancing than they were for a raft ride.

The two lesbians were in a land of their own and oblivious to everything except each other. The honeymooners looked apprehensive, but were happy in the knowledge that they would be together should any disaster strike. Melanie was excited and ready for the trip to begin as she waved her paddle in the air, and called out to Running Water, "Let's go".

The first hundred yards was tranquil as we slowly floated past strange rock formations and open caves, we practiced our paddling techniques, while Running Water issued his commands like a Marine sergeant. The first rapid was shallow but gave the raft a good pull as the water pushed us off to one side. Signs of things to come, I thought. The river here was fifty yards wide, but up ahead I could see that it narrowed to less than half that distance, I could also hear the sounds of our first large rapid.

"Paddles up" ordered Running Water.

We all took our paddles out of the water and let him control the direction of the raft through this first rapid from his position in the stern. The raft slid through the rocks and down the crest of the waves as we successfully maneuvered our way through.

"Piece of cake" I heard Melanie yell excitedly from the back of the raft.

As we came through the rapid the guide called for me to pull hard on my paddle to bring us straight in line for the next rapid. I dug deep into the churning water and pulled, the raft straightened as we entered a series of small fast moving rapids, which were followed by a much larger and swifter one. Everyone cheered as we made it through, some from exhilaration and some out of fear. The river widened and became peaceful once again.

I could hear the loud roar of a rapid ahead, and I could feel the raft begin to accelerate.

"This is the Camel coming up" called Running Water, "it's long and steep, stay alert and relax".

The water was white as far ahead as I could see as the raft crested at the top of the Camel. Soon we were being thrown from side to side as we made our way through. The guide shouted his commands to me or to the 'spy' to paddle or not paddle. It was hard work and I understood his reason for selecting us for the two important positions at the bow. We were all wet by now, and even though the water was cold and the temperature barely above sixty degrees, I was sweating.

As the raft descended the final section of the Camel I heard Running Water shouting "Port, Port".

That's me, I thought. I dug in hard and pulled with all my strength, then I dug in again and missed the water, my paddle flipped around with the force of my attempted pull and hit the 'spy' on the side of his head. He was caught off balance and fell into the raging water.

"Keep her straight" yelled the guide, as he jumped in to help the 'spy'.

The raft was now clear of the rapids and entering a placid shallow area with a sandy beach, I directed the crew to pull over to the beach, where we pulled the raft to safety. We could see two red helmets bobbing in the water, as the guide and the 'spy' swam unhurt towards the beach.

Melanie came to stand beside me; she had an accusing look on her wet face.

"It was an accident" I stammered.

"Sure it was" she stated, "he could have been injured, David".

"No harm done" I shrugged.

If he had looked ridiculous before, then now he looked really idiotic. He was being fussed over by the lesbian girls, one was drying his hair with an old worn out sweater, while her cohort was attempting to straighten his tie. The honeymooners were busily squeezing the excess water from his pants and jacket, while Running Water was explaining to us all that accidents like this are not unusual.

"See" I said.

"People call me Mac. It's short for MacDonald" replied the 'spy' in response to the lesbian's question.

I had christened the pair Butch and Bitch. I had also put names to the honeymooners but before I could tell Melanie of my choices they had introduced themselves as Helen and Jerry. They explained that they had been high school sweethearts, but had moved apart. They had both married and both had families that were now grown. Jerry was divorced and Helen's husband died, they had joined singles clubs to occupy their time and Helen had eventually located Jerry through the internet, and the rest was history.

Melanie supplied a fabricated story about our relationship that seemed to satisfy everyone's curiosity.

Running Water switched the positions on the raft of Mac and Melanie, relegating Mac to the stern of the raft; we all donned our paddling gear and launched the raft back into the water.

The river changed from brown to blue as we continued the trip through the mighty canyon, we surfed through more rapids without anymore mishaps. The river became calm once again and we had time to observe some of the wild life that made the Canyon their home. We saw a flock large birds circling overhead, while the guide directed our attention to a small group of deer drinking at the water's edge. A herd of wild goats danced across the rocks halfway up the steep sided canyon, we all watched and wondered how they kept their footing. Soon the river widened once again and we all paddled slowly towards a rocky beach which marked the end of the trip.

Lunch had been prepared for us by three Indian women who were dressed in their traditional costumes; the lunch was not as traditional as the costumes and consisted of Hamburgers, Tuna and Chicken Burgers and Hot Dogs. The food was accompanied by Budweiser or Californian White Zinfandel. The beer was ice cold, the burgers were perfectly cooked, and nothing could have been more satisfying or timely.

Helen insisted on taking a group picture. I suggested to Melanie that she pose with Butch and Bitch, while I cozied up to Mac! We had avoided any conversation or even eye contact but he knew that I had tumbled to his cover, and he was embarrassed to have to continue to play his charade. Moreover he had become the object of concern for his fellow travelers, a situation that any covert operator dreaded, a no- no in the spy operation's manual. He was stricken with fear about having his picture taken, especially with the very person that he was following; I had to give him credit for managing to obscure his face while the cameras were snapping. Photos are not my bag either.

"Send Charlie the bill for the dry cleaning" I said to Mac, "too bad about the shoes though".

He didn't respond, just gathered his wet clothes together and followed the other trippers to the waiting helicopter, with his tail between his legs. His cell phone would have been ruined in the water, so he had no means of making contact with Charlie or anybody else who may have been directing his mission.

Melanie was helping the Indian women clear the lunch dishes from the tables, I walked over to her and slipped my arms around her waist, she was taken by surprise but relaxed instantly when she realized it was me. I pulled her close and kissed the back of her neck "I've missed you" I murmured, "am I forgiven?"

"For what?"

"Dunking Mac. I thought you were mad at me?"

"I was for a moment, but it was really quite funny to see him so wet and helpless" she giggled.

"And with his fancy shoes filled with sand, and his suit still with the buttons in place" I laughed.

"I wish I had brought my camera, he was the highlight of the trip".

"I hardly touched him. Just caught him off balance"

We both continued to laugh at Mac's expense as we hiked the short distance to the helicopter.

"What a day" I said "I wonder what tomorrow will bring".

"There's never a dull moment with you David. Do you think that Charlie will show tomorrow?"

"I doubt that he will, but I wish he would, it would be easier to stay a step of him if I knew where he was, but now I'll have no idea who's watching us. He'll replace Mac, and then we're exposed again".

"You mentioned earlier that you needed his expertise and his contacts".

"I can do without him; a second opinion would have been nice".

The return flight followed the Grand Canyon westwards towards the sinking sun; the rocks were already tinted with red as the sun began to set. In the distance the lights of the Las Vegas strip were glowing in the early evening dusk.

"Just like a fairyland" Melanie commented. "I had so much fun today. Thank you David".

"You'll still have time to visit the casino".

"I don't think so, I'm exhausted. It's early to bed tonight".

I could have made a smart remark, but with our conversation anything but private in the confines of the helicopter, I held my suggestive comments to myself. I did smile a mischievous smile though, and I know that Melanie saw it.

CHAPTER NINE

I registered at the reception desk of the Convention as a foreign V.I.P., I received a red name tag, a plastic bag of advertising material, a map of the convention floor and a schedule of events. I kept the map and dumped the rest of the freebies in the first garbage container that I saw. I knew who I was looking for and I had previously checked with the front desk to make sure that my contact was registered at the hotel.

Bima Sheekato was the man I needed to find. He was from Indonesia and the only son of Prince Sheekato, who was one of the richest men in the world and the owner of Consolidated Diamond Mines of Jakarta.

Bima was my age. We had met for the first time in England at Ascot, not actually at the race track, but in the parking lot. He had locked his keys in his car with the engine running and was searching for a rock to break one of the car's windows so that he could enter his car and turn off the engine before proceeding into the races. I could see that he was very frustrated and on the point of doing something foolish. I asked him if I could help, he threw up his hands and told me to go ahead. Car doors are a 'piece of cake' to a safe cracker like me, and I had the door open in thirty seconds.

He pulled a wad of bills from his pocket and offered to pay me for my help. Of course I refused his offer but did I suggest that he put his money on White Diamond, a horse that was running in the fifth race.

We entered Ascot Park together and spent the day together. He followed my advice and won a bundle in the fifth race, then the sixth and the ninth. He insisted that I share in his good fortune, he invited me for a drink and asked if I could join him for dinner. I followed him as we entered the Grandstand where he took the private elevator to the Royal Box. My mouth was open for most of the way. Who is this fellow I wondered?

He introduced me to his mother, sister and father; I wasn't sure if I was expected to bow, shake hands or kiss the ground. Bima immediately saw my discomfort and beckoned for me to take a seat and have a drink. He explained to his family the circumstances under which we had met and the success that he had had at the betting window, all thanks to me. The family had a renewed interest in me and the father asked if I would be their guest the next day, he added that they would have to vacate the Royal Box because the Queen would be in attendance. Such a drag, I thought. I had planned to be at the races anyway, so I had nothing to lose and maybe lots to gain, it never hurts to have rich friends, and this group was as rich as it gets!

I had recognized his father from some recent pictures I had seen in the newspaper. He was the target of plenty of animosity from the rebel faction of the Indonesian people. In actual fact he was one of the largest and fairest employers in the country, he was a philanthropist and a promoter of education and health for his fellow Indonesians. I was unaware of the source of his wealth, thinking mistakenly that it was inherited from his father or came from shipping interests. It was Bima who informed me that the family was in the diamond mining business, with mines in the Kalimantan region of Indonesia, an area where the stones were mined from deep in the ground. I later learned that the diamonds from this area were formed by unusually high pressure in strata within hard black coal, and that they were among the most desirable stones in the world.

The evening I spent with Bima was an education for me, even though I had thought that I would be giving him one. He had two goals in his young life, to see how much he could drink and to see how many girls he could nail. I tagged along as he dragged me from pub to pub, then from club to club, and everywhere we went he ordered expensive champagne for any girl that showed even the slightest interest in us. I was becoming drunk and concerned for his safety, but he would not listen to my warnings. However I did convince him to lock his car, and take a taxi home rather than drive and I had only achieved this small concession but stealing his keys and conveniently losing them. I don't remember where I went to bed or with whom, but I do remember the headache I awoke with the following morning.

The race card on Derby day was a handicapper's nightmare with too many unknowns racing, or horses that were imported or returning from long lay offs. I told Bima and his family that they would be wise to keep their money in their pockets, which is exactly what I did.

I had remained in contact with Bima over the years, he was now married with three small children, and I was looking forward to reuniting with him at the convention.

My concern was Charlie. I could not afford to have a meeting with Bima while Charlie or one of his 'spies' was tailing me. I had disposed of Mac, but I was certain that there were others whose job assignment was to keep me under observation. I knew that I was not in danger, as Charlie was not a violent crook, and our 'friendship' did count for something. I had to find a way to contact Bima without out meeting looking anything more than a casual re-acquaintance.

I entered the main convention floor where the crowds of eager traders were already wheeling and dealing. It was here that you could trade for almost everything and anything that you could imagine. The floor itself had been divided into sections to make locating the product or service that you were interested in easier to find. There was a Real Estate section, Automotive section, Valuables section, Vacation section and on and on. I headed in the direction of the valuables section, knowing that Bima or someone from his company would be there.

It was like a homecoming reunion for me, I had not realized how many people that I knew would be in attendance. I shook hands or hugged dozens of old friends and exchanged greetings with lots more. All of this worked to my advantage as Charlie's observer would find it extremely difficult to identify all these individuals, so I made a point of greeting as many as I could, some that I hardly knew at all.

A pretty young Asian girl was handing out pamphlets from beneath an Indonesian flag. I approached her when she was alone.

"Do you work for Consolidated?" I asked.

"Yes sir", she answered.

"Is Bima Sheekato here?"

"I think he's having breakfast. But he'll be back soon".

I extracted a business card from my wallet and scribbled a note on the back. I handed the card to the girl.

"Please make sure he gets this message, and tell him that it's very important", I said.

The message I had written was quite simple:-

> *Tee off time 2 pm. today at Thunderbird.*
> *Bring a fourth……David.*

Bima was an avid golfer, and I knew that he would not pass up the opportunity to play at the famous Thunderbird Golf and Country Club.

Even if one of Charlie's observers followed me to the golf course, there was no way they could follow me around the course in a golf cart. And having a foursome precluded the chance of a stranger being assigned to play with us.

Melanie was on a shopping spree, spending her winnings, she had said that she would be somewhere in the hotel's boutique gallery while I attended the convention. I found her shopping for shoes. She was so engrossed in her search for exactly the right pair that she never saw me enter the store. I walked up behind her.

"Check to see if they have any golf shoes" I told her.

She looked up in surprise with a smile on her face. I could see that she was happy, women love to shop.

"Golf shoes?" she asked.

"We tee off at two", I answered.

"Are you serious? Golf?"

"You do play?"

"About as well as I ski" she answered with a grin.

"I'll tell you why during lunch. Are you nearly finished here?"

"What do you think of these?" she asked as she slipped on a pair of high heeled evening shoes.

I knew better than to ask the price, anyway it was her money.

"I like them" I said.

"Me too. I just hope I get the chance to wear them. I'll take them" she said to the sales girl "I'm done".

Over lunch I told her about my concern over being shadowed by Charlie's 'spies'.

"I'm sure that we're being watched at this very moment. Take a look around, it could be anyone of the other patrons in this place or it could be someone watching from outside. I'm not being paranoid".

She looked at the customers at the other tables before she spoke "They all look suspicious to me. How can we expose them?"

"We'll have to lose them before we play golf. We are meeting an old friend of mine at the golf course.

Once we are on the course we'll be fine, but getting there unseen is the problem".

"Can I ask you who we're playing with and why?"

"An old friend of mine named Bima Sheekato. He's from Indonesia. His father is a real Prince and owns one of the largest diamond mining companies in the world. Bima's a golf fanatic and the golf course will be the ideal place for me to conclude the next phase of my plan. But Charlie mustn't know".

"So we lose him or her on the way".

"Correct, but easier said than done".

"I'm sure you've done this sort of thing before" she said.

I had an idea how we could evade our observers without putting ourselves at risk. My intuition told me that he would have two 'spies' watching us, one tailing me and one tailing Melanie. When we were together, as we were right now, it would give one of them the chance to report in or to take a break. If we left the hotel together, then the chance was that only one of them would be watching. Losing one would be much easier than losing two.

"We'll leave together by taxi. We'll stop by a golf shop to buy shoes, and then we'll come back here. We'll stop off at the front of the hotel, walk directly through the lobby, past the boutiques and the pool area and then out to the garage where we will have another taxi waiting. We'll be on our way to the golf course in a flash. What do you think?"

"It sounds like a good plan to me" she said, "But are we really going to play golf?"

"Yes we are. We'll rent clubs at the pro shop. I asked Bima to bring a partner; it could be his wife or his sister. I'm sorry but you'll be stuck with who ever he brings in your golf cart".

"It's Ok. White water rafting one day and golfing with royalty the next. I can't wait for tomorrow".

We arrived at the Thunderbird Golf Club in high spirits. The plan had worked to a tee, if anybody had been watching us, then we had definitely eluded them. The mad dash through the lobby had raised some eyebrows, but not those of our watch dogs. I felt quite safe from Charlie, and was looking forward to my meeting with Bima.

Melanie was fitting herself out in the pro shop, when I saw her I had to comment.

"If you play half as good as you look, you'll be a sensation".

"You might be in for a surprise" she winked.

Bima almost ran into my arms when he saw me as I was leaving the pro shop "David, David" he kept repeating, "this is a wonderful surprise".

We hugged one another and slapped each others backs like long lost brothers; he still looked about nineteen, although he had filled out a little. I introduced him to Melanie, she smiled and actually curtsied, and then he introduced us to the pretty girl who had been giving away the pamphlets at his booth. Her name was Lyn Lee.

"Lyn is my golf teacher" he explained.

Sure I thought, just like Melanie is my lawyer. We men are such shallow creatures, why can't we just be honest and tell each other that we are being unfaithful, instead of acting out this pretense.

"Melanie is a lawyer" I proclaimed in aloud voice "but she's also my girlfriend. We make passionate love every night, and she's the best thing that's ever happened to me".

We all laughed to ease the tension that my remark had caused.

Melanie smiled and added "He's not kidding; we just can't keep our hands off one another".

"How's your wife?" I asked innocently.

"Pregnant again" Bima replied, "it must be something in the water".

"How many will this be?"

"Five and that's it".

"He had a vasectomy, yesterday" whispered Lyn, loud enough for us all to hear. "I hope it doesn't affect his swing".

Her comment sounded so out of place that we all laughed harder than the remark warranted.

We drove to the practice area to hit a few balls before teeing off. I watched as Lyn hit a nine iron with the grace of a professional, she really could be his golf teacher.

Just to make the game interesting we decided to place a small wager on each hole, the lowest aggregate score of the two players comprising each team would win. Ten dollars per hole was agreed upon as the amount of the bet, and at Melanie's suggestion the teams were to be the boys against the girls. I had already conceded that the best player was Lyn, I knew that Bima was better than average, I was below average, and Melanie was an unknown. On paper it looked like a fair arrangement. Lyn and Melanie occupied one cart while the two men had the other.

Thunderbird is a long course from the blue tees, so it was agreed that the men and Lyn would play from the white tees and Melanie would play from the ladies tees.

Lyn drove first, to a look of envy from me, as we all watched her ball travel at least 240 yards straight down the middle of the fairway. Bima's ball was as long off the tee but it found the short rough to the left, while my drive only traveled about 125 yards. I was embarrassed by my short drive, but at least it was straight. The ladies tee, where Melanie was taking a few practice swings was approximately 25 yards ahead of the white tees. She selected a three wood from her bag and addressed her ball. I was tempted to suggest that she should use the driver but refrained at the last moment, which saved me considerable embarrassment as she out drove us all with a picture perfect drive.

"We're in serious trouble Bima" I said, "this will be a costly day, not to our pocket books but to our prides".

The girls won the first five holes easily, as I recall Lyn was at even par while Melanie was one over, they actually had the audacity to suggest that we rearrange the teams to make the game more interesting. It was a day of humiliation. At the completion of the front nine, they had won eight holes while one was tied. We decided to stop for a break at the clubhouse. While the girls went off giggling their way to the ladies room, I ordered two bottles of champagne from the bar. I was hoping that getting them tipsy would provide us with the slight edge that we needed. It was evident that they both had hollow legs, because they consumed more than us and showed no ill effects at all, and in fact it was my game that degenerated. We were skunked on the back nine!

"Is there anything you can't do" I asked.

Without hesitation Melanie replied "Skate backwards; play the violin; keep a secret; be faithful".

"Touché!" I laughed.

"A private joke" I explained to Bima.

The two girls who had found a common friendship based on their superiority over us at golf, departed for the ladies shower, leaving me an opportunity to broach the subject of a deal with Bima.

I reached into my bag and extracted a glossy brochure describing the 'Princess'. I had found several of these very exquisite brochures in one of the lockers on board the yacht; I had assumed that they had been produced by the manufacturer as give-a ways for any prospective buyers that came to view the boat at the boat shows in Florida. 'Princess' had been their flag ship, their show boat, the boat that they had hoped would lead to additional sales. I handed the brochure to Bima.

He flipped through the pages quickly before asking "Why am I looking at this?"

"I thought it would make a nice gift for your father's anniversary".

He laughed, and then asked, "Who's the owner?"

"I am".

"David, don't joke with me".

"It's true, it's mine and I want to trade it to you for your best diamonds".

"You can't be serious".

"I am Bima. Very serious. The yacht is on its way to Bermuda, she should arrive tomorrow. We can inspect her anytime".

"But diamonds? How will you dispose of them? We are having trouble ourselves".

"I have a customer, don't worry about that. Can we make a deal?"

"It's possible, David, but we are friends and I hope we will remain so for a long time. This kind of trade could turn us against one another, and having said that, I'm willing to be straightforward and put my cards on the table and be realistic about relative values".

"I understand exactly what you are saying, but here's what I have in mind. The value of this yacht is between ten and twelve million dollars. The selling price of a yacht such as this is established by the manufacturer and will vary according to the customization that the buyer specifies at the time of its manufacture. I'm sure you'll do your homework, but I can assure you that those are the true facts".

"I have no doubt that you are correct, and I will check, but for now I'll accept your valuation. Let's talk diamonds".

"Bima, I do know something about diamonds, not as much as you but I'm not a fool. I'll trade the yacht for diamonds with a retail value of one hundred million dollars. They must be larger than 1 carat, be colour D, the clarity should be VVS1 or FL, and the cut must be Round Brilliant".

He made no comment. He reached into his pocket and withdrew a small black velvet bag which he passed across the table to me. "Take a look at those" he said.

I tipped the contents of the bag into my hand. There were six stones glistening in the palm of my hand.

Bima handed me a small magnifying glass. "Tell me if they would suit you?"

He continued to speak as I studied the stones under the magnifying glass.

"They are 2 carats each, Flawless, some of the prettiest and most valuable stones we have ever produced. Each stone is worth between 200 and 250 thousand dollars. If you rotate them in your fingers you'll appreciate their remarkable make".

I knew that the make of a stone referred to its cut.

"These are beautiful. Do you have more?"

"Yes, we have more, but let me say again, it will be almost impossible to sell stones of this value on the market. The DeBeens family of South Africa controls the sale of diamonds world wide and no retailer can afford to buy outside of their control. They would be cut off and out of business if they tried".

"Do you have five hundred stones just like these?"

"I'm sure that we have. You're figuring the value at 10 percent of retail?"

"Yes, do you agree that that's fair?"

"I'd say it's closer to 15 percent, but let's not haggle right now. Put these stones in your pocket, scrutinize them at your leisure tonight, I will talk to my father by telephone and advise him of our tentative agreement. Then we'll meet again tomorrow".

"You'll trust me with these jewels?"

"Of course, but as I've said, you'll have difficulty selling them".

"Keep the brochure. The yacht comes with a crew of three and a Captain; they're very capable and pleasant people".

We shook hands as if we had concluded the deal. I carefully rewrapped the stones into the little bag and put them safely into my pocket. Bima folded the brochure and slid it into a side pocket of his golf bag.

"Let's go shower" I suggested, "before the girls return".

I stood under the shower to let the water cascade over my head while I mentally reexamined the terms of the deal I had made with Bima. If my mathematics was correct then five hundred stones at twenty thousand dollars each came to a total of ten million dollars, and if the value of some of the stones was somewhat higher then the final total could be closer to twelve million. I pinched myself to make sure that I wasn't dreaming. For a small time scoundrel this was an unbelievable coup. But I still had to sell the stones.

My immediate problem was still Charlie, his surveillance and his ultimate intention. It was quite obvious that Melanie had found a friend in Lyn; she also knew that Bima was one of my oldest friends, so it didn't take a mind reader to speculate that at this very moment they were planning an evening together for the four of us. There was no polite way that I could squelch such an evening without alienating all of them. I could tell them the truth, or part of it, let them know of my concern over Charlie, or I could ignore the threat and act naturally. If Charlie received a report from one of his operatives that I was having dinner with Bima, what could he do? Would he surmise that I was

145

exchanging the Bahamian dollars for diamonds, not likely, Bima would have no use for them? He would have no idea that the currency had already been exchanged, unless he had been able to discover the truth of the yacht purchase from a source within the Bahamas.

As predicted, the four of us were scheduled to have dinner later, and then to go dancing at one of the many discos in town. By the time I had returned to our table in the club bar, the plans had been made.

"Sounds like a plan to me" I said with fake enthusiasm. "I'll dust off my dancing shoes".

Melanie had informed Bima that we had arrived at the Golf Club in a taxi, so he had insisted that we drive back to the hotel in his limo. We had 'one for the road' at the loser's expense of course, before loading all our paraphernalia into the limo and driving back to town.

Sealed into a special compartment in one of my suitcases was high magnification inspection glass. To really examine a diamond it is essential that a magnification of at lest ten times normal be employed. Higher magnification provides no additional benefit as the sole purpose is to detect flaws, and these are easily seen with the ten times glass. I had the six stones on the bureau with a desk light shining directly over them. As I examined each one from many different angles, it became very clear to me that Bima was correct in his valuation. These stones were truly exceptional. I heard Melanie singing in the bedroom and couldn't resist the temptation of showing her the jewels.

"Melanie" I called "I've got something to show you".

"I'm coming" she answered.

She came over to the desk to see what it was that I was studying.

"Oh my God" she exclaimed when she saw them.

"Beautiful little baubles, aren't they?'

"David, they're magnificent. Can I touch them?"

I picked one from the group and placed it in her hand. She turned it over and over and finally asked "how much?'

"A quarter of a million" I answered casually.

"For just one?"

"Look at it with this" I said as I handed her the magnifying glass, "you may never ever see a better diamond than this. Look at the cut, the clarity, the colour and the absence of any inclusions or flaws. You don't need to be an expert to see how perfect they are".

"I'm scared that I may drop it" she said, "are they legal. I mean they're not stolen or anything?"

"No, they belong to Bima, actually to Consolidated Mines. He said I could hold on to them until we conclude our transaction".

"There are more of these?"

"I've offered him the 'Princess' for five hundred of them. What do you think?"

Her brain quickly calculated the total amount.

"That's a hundred and twenty five million" she gasped.

"And I'll get about ten percent of that for them. Not bad eh!"

"I don't know what to say. Let me sit down, my legs are weak. I can't believe that you were walking around with these in your pocket. There's more than a million dollars there".

"Bima actually had them in his pocket while we were playing golf!"

"Let's give them back to him at dinner; I won't be able to sleep if you still have them in your pocket. Suppose you lost them, or they were stolen. Please give them back".

"How will you carry five hundred of them if just six terrify you?" I laughed.

"Me?" she exclaimed "I could never carry them?"

"Don't bet on it" I said seriously.

"What do you mean?"

"If I complete the deal with Bima, we will probably have to fly to Bermuda to make the trade. Naturally he'll want to inspect the yacht before he parts with the diamonds."

"Fly to Bermuda?" she interrupted with incredulity, "when?"

"Day after tomorrow, most likely. Is that a problem?"

"David, I just can't keep up with you, I'm exhausted just thinking about all this. And now Bermuda?"

"Then London", I added.

"Can we stop off in Paris or Monte Carlo, while we're so close?"

"Paris? No. But Monte Carlo is a definite possibility" I said.

"Seriously, are we going to London?

"With five hundred of these little baubles in our pockets".

"Oh, my God. I'll just die".

"Nah" I smiled "It'll be a 'piece of cake'"

CHAPTER TEN

Bima's private jet circled the Bermuda International airport before making the final approach to the runway. Our flight had been uneventful since the departure from Las Vegas, but more importantly for me was the knowledge that I was beyond Charlie's reach. Even if he had been notified of my association with Bima, there would have been no way for him to learn of our destination. A check of our flight plan would have only yielded the information that we were headed to Los Angeles; somehow Bima had been able to provide an alternative plan and conceal our actual destination.

During dinner last night I had taken Bima into my confidence by telling him of my concern over Charlie's intentions, I did not mention to him any of the details regarding the procurement of the yacht, nor the source of the funds for its purchase. All through dinner Melanie could talk of nothing but the diamonds, it was only after they were returned to their rightful owner that she began to relax and enjoy herself. I thought that it was an interesting observation that nobody at the table wore diamonds, unless Lyn had one in her navel!

I asked her while we were dancing. For a moment she must have thought that she hadn't heard me correctly because she looked at me in a peculiar fashion, then began to giggle "I'm not sure I should answer that question".

149

"Then I'll take it as a yes" I said.

"No, no" she pleaded "I don't, but I have one someplace else!"

Unfortunately the music ended right about then, so I never did find out the diamond's location. My fertile imagination was only able to come up with three possibilities.

Bima had never met a bright, intelligent and capable girl like Melanie, he was used to either bimbos or Indonesian girls who were not permitted to pursue careers in those professions reserved exclusively for men. I could tell by his body language while he was dancing with her, that he was uncomfortable, except for their social status they were on equal footing, in fact she was probably way ahead of him in many areas. I wondered if she would pick his pocket, I was tempted, and had it been a different time and place, I probably would have, after all he had a fortune in stones in his pocket.

I drank too much; but then I was on a high, today had been a monumental day in my life, I was close to becoming a multimillionaire, so close that I could taste it. How I retained my composure I don't know, I had an urge to go wild, to scream at the top of my voice, to dance on the table tops, to whirl around the dance floor in a frenzy; but I didn't. But I made a promise to myself that I would.

"I wanna go back to the hotel and make love to you" I whispered in Melanie's ear as we danced close to a romantic ballad.

"We can't leave yet".

"I bet they wanna do the same".

"Do you really think that they're lovers?"

"Love has nothing to do with it" I said drunkenly.

"I love you when you're tipsy" she giggled.

"But not when I'm sober?"

"Yes, sober too".

"You're taller than him, I noticed when you were both dancing" I slurred my words but continued "his nose was level with your tits. He was talking to them".

I began to laugh at my own humour, a bad sign, I knew that I would only become worse, but I carried on undaunted.

"Hi left tit, my name's Bima. I'm sorry did I ignore you righty?"

"David, stop".

"I saw his lips moving, he must've been saying somethin'"

"To me, not to these" she demonstrated by pulling herself hard against me.

"Take me home, please" I implored her. "I'm horny".

Somehow she managed to extricate us from the restaurant without offending our dinner partners; I kissed her tenderly on the lips as the taxi sped back to the Riviera Hotel.

"I like neckin' in the back seat" I said.

"Me too" she purred.

"I'm so exhilarated, I can hardly contain myself" I admitted.

"I may have a cure for that".

"You say the darndest things. I can't imagine what you mean".

We staggered through the lobby on the way to the elevator. I was the one who was staggering; Melanie was merely lending support.

"Floor, sir?" inquired the elevator attendant"

"Ok, that'll be fine" I replied as I settled onto the floor of the elevator, folded my arms under my head to form a pillow and closed my eyes.

We eventually made it to our suite with no more incidents. I remember standing in the shower, but I have no recollection of getting undressed. But I remember vividly the sensuous creature that slipped naked into the shower with me.

"Hello beautiful titties" I joked "and beautiful shoulders, and beautiful belly, and beautiful thighs, and beautiful..." I stopped to laugh and to clear my face from the water, "I don't know a polite name for this part of your anatomy, but whatever it's called I love it. It's so soft and fluffy, like a little fluffy kitten, I'm gonna call it my pussy".

"But you can't, 'cause it's mine".

"Can we share it?" I asked in a childlike voice.

"Oh sure, she loves attention".

I lavished attention on my new found friend; the response was wonderful and led to all kinds of exciting new experiences for both of us. A friend in deed is a friend in need, or is it the other way around.

The following morning I placed a call to Jeremy on board 'Princess'. I needed to know if he had arrived in Bermuda, and whether he had encountered any suspicious behavior from any over enthusiastic customs official.

"We arrived yesterday, cleared immigration and customs without a hitch" he stated "will you be arriving anytime soon?"

"Sooner than expected" I told him "tomorrow, to be exact with two or three guests. They may decide to stay in a hotel instead of on board, but you should be prepared to accommodate them if they accept my offer of the yacht's staterooms. Incidentally if you are contacted by Charles Wolfsen, either by phone or by messenger or in person, under no circumstance should you allow him or his agent to board. He may try to convince you that we are best friends and that I have extended an open invitation for him to visit me, but nothing could be further from the truth. He's not welcome".

"Message received loud and clear, Boss" he acknowledged.

"How was your trip?"

"Smooth and very pleasant, the weather was good and the sea quite calm. We made good time".

"I'm glad. How's the Yacht Club?"

"Very British, we have the best slip on the outside dock, it's nice here".

"I'll see you tomorrow sometime".

Evidently we had agreed last night to have breakfast with Bima and Lyn this morning, luckily for me Melanie had been capable of remembering, because I had no recollection of such an arrangement.

They were waiting for us when we entered the cafeteria, sipping coffee with their heads together in a secretive conversation.

"I bet they're talking about me" I whispered to Melanie.

"Probably" she agreed "you were the highlight of the evening".

"I feel terrible".

"A good breakfast will work wonders".

"Ugh!" I groaned.

After a round of 'Good Mornings' and 'great time last night' comments, I ordered some scrambled eggs, toast and sausage. The morning tea was already easing my hangover, as my mother used to say "there's nothin' like a good cuppa".

Bima had talked at length to his father, who was in New York for a meeting at the United Nations, and he had decided to meet us in Bermuda. This was excellent news, not only would he have the opportunity of inspecting 'Princess' first hand, but he would also be able to complete the deal in short order. Bima explained to us that the function that his father performed with the United Nations was in the establishment of the 'Kimberley Process', a process to eliminate or control what had come to be known in the industry, as conflict diamonds.

The term 'conflict diamonds' is now widely used to describe diamonds that are mined or stolen to provide funds for armed rebellion against legitimate, internationally recognized governments.

The term originated in 1998 with the imposition by the United Nations Security Council of political and economic sanctions on the Angolan Rebel Group, UNITA. The sanctions covered diamonds mined by UNITA from riverbed deposits under its control.

Since then, rebels in Sierra Leone and the Democratic Republic of the Congo have also been charged with funding their conflicts through the sale of diamonds.

The diamond industry has taken upon itself the task of policing the sale of diamonds, by enforcing a requirement that ensures that all diamonds offered for sale are accompanied by certifiable warranties.

Although these 'conflict diamonds' only account for three or four per cent of all diamond sales, the industry's concern is that the buying public will refrain from purchasing diamonds if they think that their purchases are financing rebels.

"So David", Bima joked, "my father wants to be sure that you're not a rebel planning to overthrow the legitimate government of your country?"

"The problem with governments" I said "is that even if you can get rid of one, another takes its place, probably just as bad as the first one. I'll leave politics to someone else".

"My father also asked me to check into the documentation of the yacht. I assume that you are in possession of the necessary papers. I trust you David, but there's a lot at stake so we must be certain".

"I understand completely, my lawyer prepared the documents and had them duly executed. Everything is kosher. Just ask her, she's sitting next to you!"

Melanie explained how the transaction had taken place in the Bahamas, and that the vessel continued to have Bahamian registration. This she advised had some distinct advantages to a foreign buyer, depending upon the regulations that existed in that persons own country. She confessed that she had no knowledge of the pertinent Indonesian laws, but suggested that Bima's father would know. She informed us that documentation was limited to vessels owned by American Citizens or corporations and was a function controlled by the United States Coast Guard.

I could see that Bima was impressed by Melanie's familiarity with the subject.

"And you thought she was just a pretty face" I kidded him.

"Now I understand why you invited her along. I totally misunderstood" he said sarcastically "silly me".

Our departure had been scheduled for twelve noon, which had meant that we had needed to check out of the hotel by ten. Lyn had decided to stay in Las Vegas until the convention ended, so the flight to Bermuda had been just for the three of us. It was clear to me that Bima did not want his father to know about his affair with his 'golf teacher', or if he did know he didn't want to flaunt her in his father's face.

Bermuda reminded me of Spanish Wells, there was a similarity to the people's accents, and I noticed they must have purchased their colourful house paints from the same discount store, because all the house were painted as brightly as those in Spanish Wells. Here to, the majority of the local population derived its livelihood from the sea and they to possessed that same old salty weather beaten look as the folks in Spanish Wells.

Melanie had noticed the sameness.

"This feels like home" she said, with a sigh of contentment.

"Island life agrees with you".

"I suppose so; I'm just not a big city girl".

I had extended an invitation to Bima and his father to stay on 'Princess' while they were here, after all it would be theirs soon.

"I think I should stay with my father, David" Bima explained "he has a reservation at the Hamilton Marriott, and he'll want me to be with him. You do understand?"

"What time do you expect him?" Melanie asked "and I hate to ask you this, but how do I address him".

Bima laughed at the question.

"Your Highness will be fine" he joked, "I'm sure that once you have been introduced to him, he'll ask you to call him Joe. That's his name; I know that you'll like him. He said that he would leave New York after lunch, he could be here already".

Our taxi pulled into the driveway of the Marriott Hotel to drop off Bima before continuing on to the Yacht Club.

"Please come in with me" said Bima "while I check to see if my father has arrived. He'll be disappointed if he has to wait until later this evening to meet with you. You can find another cab".

I paid the taxi and asked the driver to take our bags to the Yacht Club.

I followed Melanie and Bima into the hotel lobby, where Bima was making inquiries at the front desk. In response to his questions the receptionist pointed to the bar that was located off to the left of lobby, indicating that was where his father was waiting.

As we entered I heard him before I caught sight of him, because he let out a roar as he saw Bima lead us into the bar.

He was a handsome man, taller than his son, and even though I knew that he must be at least fifty five years of age, he could easily pass for forty. He looked younger than me! He had black hair that was turning gray, it gave him a distinguished look that suited him and high lighted the chiseled features of his face. He was seated at a small table with a beautiful lady, who now sat in silence as Bima's father jumped up to hug his son. Bima extricated himself from his father's embrace and made the introductions.

"Please call me Joe" he said to Melanie, much to her obvious relief.

"David, it's been a long time, too long in fact".

He pumped my hand in a vigorous shake and then hugged me. "You've done well I see" he commented, as he winked in Melanie's direction.

"I'd like you both to meet Jasmine" he said, as the beautiful lady at the table was introduced to us, "Jasmine is Bima's new mother!"

"He only says that to annoy Bima. We've been married for almost a month now, but he just can't resist making a joke" Jasmine commented.

"Congratulations" I said with a wink "you've done equally as well I see".

He enjoyed my ribbing and bellowed with laughter, I doubt that he ever did anything quietly. His joviality was infectious and as Bima had said it would be difficult not to like him. Melanie was already overwhelmed by his exuberance, she accepting his offer of a drink and settling into a conversation with Jasmine.

"Tell me about the boat, David" Joe asked.

"It's a yacht, Father, not a boat" his son corrected him.

"Whatever. She's here?"

"Arrived yesterday from Nassau" I stated, "you're welcome to see her anytime. We could have dinner on board if you'd like?"

"That would be fun. You're sure?"

"I insist, I only have to make a call to the captain".

"Here Dad, look at this" Bima handed his father one of the glossy brochures.

Joe took his time as he studied every page; finally he passed the brochure to Jasmine.

"Here's your belated wedding present" he announced "it's even got your name on it".

He laughed so loudly at his own joke that we all had to join in. I thought it was quite amusing and one look at Melanie and I knew that she too had realized the significance of the yacht's name.

"I'd like to have a survey done".

"You should, I would feel more comfortable if you did. I checked the yacht's logs and maintenance records very thoroughly before I bought her, but a survey wasn't performed. I think it would be a good idea".

"Does she have the capability of traveling to Europe?"

"Yes. Extra fuel capacity was incorporated when she was built, as I recall her range is three thousand miles".

Joe motioned for me to join him away from the table, out of ear shot of Jasmine and Melanie.

"David, I have to be certain of one thing" he said seriously "and if I'm not satisfied with your answer, then the deal will be off".

I knew what was coming but answered calmly "Go ahead, ask".

"You must understand that these stones are of extremely high quality, so high that they are difficult to sell at their true value. Now of course you could sell them at a huge discount, there's always someone out there who will buy them, but this would upset the market and jeopardize our position in that market. I cannot allow this to happen. I must be sure that you will dispose of them at the correct price, and frankly I don't know how you will achieve this".

"You place me in a difficult position" I said, "I understand your need to know how I plan to dispose of the stones, but please understand that my buyer has sworn me to secrecy. It is a legitimate sale made at the correct price. The stones will be marketed through some of the best and famous retail outlets in the world".

"But that can only be achieved through DeBeens!"

"Is that a question?" I asked.

"No, I know that they won't buy them. I've already tried".

"I have no comment. You have my word and that's all I can give you".

Joe thought about my answer for a while, then asked,

"How long after you have the stones in your possession will their sale be completed?"

"A matter of days, that's all".

"Then here is what I propose. We will complete our transaction. The yacht's papers will be properly executed and placed into a local lawyer's trust. You will complete the sale of the stones to your buyer, and if you are successful, you will instruct the lawyer to release the papers to me. If however your buyer reneges on the deal then we take the stones back and the yacht's papers are torn up".

He knew that if I had trouble selling the stones in a few days, I would never be able to sell them at all. He was prepared to give me the opportunity to prove that I could complete my side of the deal. It was fair to both sides. I held out my hand to Joe. He grasped it and shook it with his usual enthusiasm.

"Let's join the ladies and have a drink, you must remember that I'm a newly wed and I mustn't ignore my bride" he teased.

My assessment of my position had changed from the moment that I discovered that Joe was recently remarried. With a new, pretty young wife, even a man of his stature and experience became a fool. It was apparent to me that he had discussed the acquisition of the yacht with Jasmine, probably made her a promise while they were in bed, that they would indulge themselves in a romantic cruise to the Greek Islands or some other equally appetizing place. And now he couldn't go back on his promise which bade well for me. This was probably a side of his father that Bima had never witnessed, and during our serious discussion I had sensed some hostility between them. I'm sure the new wife and 'mother' had been a difficult pill for him to swallow.

I excused myself and went to phone Jeremy. He would need time to shop for dinner, and the crew would need time to spruce up the yacht for Joe's inspection. I told him to expect six for dinner, there was always the chance that Bima would find a date, I also clued him in as to who the guests would include.

"A real Princess? Wow, that'll be a first" he commented.

I decided that the time to tell Jeremy of the impending sale would be after dinner, on a face to face basis. It should be welcome news for all the crew as I was sure that Joe would treat them royally, far better than I would have been able to.

"Should we use the monogrammed dinner settings?" he asked.

"Sure, they'll get a kick out of it".

"Is there any kind of food you would prefer?"

"I'll leave it in your capable hands, we're probably limited in supplies by the short notice, but I'm sure that you'll do fine. We should be on board in an hour or so and the guests should arrive at six. Dinner at eight sounds about right. Don't you think?"

"We'll be ready, Boss!"

I relayed the schedule of events to my friends in the bar. A waiter handed me a drink as I squeezed into a chair next to Melanie, the drink was in a tall glass, amber in colour with lots of ice. I took a good slug.

"Delicious. What is it?"

"It's the local favorite, called a Dark'n Stormy" said Joe.

"What's in it?"

"Gosling's Dark Rum and Ginger Beer"

"Am I the only one drinking this?" I asked as I looked at the selection of glasses on the table.

"We thought that you would be the only one capable of handling it" commented Melanie.

"Have you tasted one?" I asked.

"It looks strong".

"Here have a sip, it's really good".

Melanie drank a little, and with a little coaching so did Jasmine. They both approved. Almost immediately five Dark'n Stormys appeared on the table as if by magic. This Joe was a prince of a guy.

We sat at the table for almost an hour listening to Joe relay stories of his escapades from when he was a young man; he was amusing to listen to and not at all what one would imagine a prince to be. We finally escaped into a taxi that our waiter had hailed for us and departed for the Yacht Club.

The taxi traveled along Front Street to Albuoy's Point where the Yacht club was located. 'Princess' was easily visible from the taxi as she glistened at the dock in the late afternoon sun.

"I almost regret having to part with her" I said.

"You're sure that the deal will go through?"

"Oh yes, I have no doubt. Why? Did you hear something to the contrary?"

"Jasmine confided in me, she mentioned that both Joe and Bima had serious doubts about your ability to sell the diamonds".

"Really, that's interesting. They'll be in for a surprise. What did you think of the new wife?"

"I liked them both, they are enjoying each other. Did you know that Jasmine was a famous movie star, she told me that she had made more than forty movies in Asia?"

"She's certainly pretty enough".

"They make a handsome couple".

"They're probably saying the same about us right about now".

Jeremy had everything under control. Dinner would be served in the formal dining room, cocktails would be served on the aft deck, and if the weather was not cooperative or if it was too cool for the ladies, then we could come inside to the main salon.

The vessel was immaculate both inside and out, the varnished wood on the hand rails shone, the stainless steel fittings were polished, the decks were scrubbed and inside she resembled a picture from an interior designer's catalogue. I congratulated Jeremy and the crew on a superb job.

"While I have you all in one place" I started out "I want to tell you about our guests. They are Prince and Princess Sheekato of Indonesia and his son Bima Sheekato, the son may bring a friend; I'm not sure about that. They are more than just rich guests, they will most likely be your new bosses. I'm planning to sell 'Princess' to them. I honestly believe that this will be wonderful news for you all, they want you all to stay and they have extensive cruising plans for the yacht. And working for Royalty will make you the envy of the other yacht crews. I know I don't have to remind you that this evening is very important, I'm sure you will all perform your duties admirably".

"Do you have any idea of their immediate plans?" asked Jeremy.

"He asked me about her range; my guess is that he'll want to cruise to Europe, maybe Monte Carlo or Nice?"

"Has he had other yachts?"

"I don't think so, this will be his first. You'll have to educate him!"

"It sounds too good to be true. We'll be on our best behavior this evening".

I found Melanie in the master stateroom looking distraught at her reflection in the full length mirror located behind the bathroom door.

"I have nothing to wear" she bleated "Jasmine will look like the Queen of Sheba and I'll look like one of her slave girls!"

"I always preferred the slave girls myself" I commented.

"Be serious David, look at me".

"I am, you're beautiful, no matter what you wear. Jasmine is a real life Princess, a movie star now married to one of the richest men in the world, we can't compete with them nor do we need to, we are who we are, and you'll be just fine".

"I wish that you had told me that we would be entertaining royalty before we left Harbour Island".

"You wouldn't have believed me, and if you had, you wouldn't have come".

"The only things I've got are those new shoes".

"That's a start. That sexy dress you wore in Nassau will knock Joe's eyes out".

"It's all I have" she said forlornly.

The crew had dressed for the occasion in their 'dress' uniforms. They served cocktails and hors d'ouvres on the aft deck as planned, the weather remained delightful, which allowed everyone ample time to enjoy the spectacular view of Hamilton. Joe insisted that we all take a tour of the yacht before dinner, as he rightfully presumed that we would be less enthusiastic after dinner. They were all overwhelmed by both her size and the quality of the interior furnishings, they could find nothing that didn't appeal to them, and even the soft colour scheme suited their taste. The massive engines and the two generators impressed Joe. He walked between the engines inspecting them for signs of oil leaks or some sign of neglect. The engine room was lit by eight fluorescent lights under whose glare the smallest smear of grime or oil could easily be detected, but there was none to find.

"She's beautiful. I'm very impressed" exclaimed Joe as he ascended the steps up to the bridge. "This looks like the cockpit of a seven forty seven".

"She's well equipped" I interjected "with two of everything".

Jasmine who was dressed very conservatively in a simple but expensive white suit, finally uttered "I think it's so exciting to own a yacht, and this one is perfect".

My sentiments exactly, I almost said, but decided to let her comment sit on Joe's conscience unqualified.

If they had been impressed with the yacht, then the dinner, the service and the decorations literally blew them away. It goes without saying that Joe had been accustomed to the best things in life, but he could not find the words to describe the dinner that evening. I

166

felt very proud of Jeremy and the crew, and after dinner was completed I ask them all to come and join us for a night cap and to be introduced to Jasmine and Joe. It was an extraordinary precedent, according to Jeremy, but then I'm an extraordinary person I told him.

Each place setting had its own individually printed menu, listing the courses, the choices and those selections which were of local interest. The menus had been printed on gold edged parchment, each with a gold tassel hanging from its upper corner with the guests name attached.

The place settings featured fine china plates, bowls, crystal glasses, silverware and napkins, all with the 'Princess' monogram. I watched my guests' eyes as they surveyed the whole area, happy in the knowledge that they were all speechless. Overhead a crystal chandelier cast a soft warm glow, while on the table, candles, each in its own monogrammed candle holder, shed a romantic light.

The food was indescribable, original and unusual. The wine selection was equally as perfect. For once Joe was silent as he savored this incredible feast.

It was Bima who broke the silence with a toast to the chef, as we all raised our wine glasses and joined in the toast.

"Who is the chef?" asked Jasmine in a loud voice.

Jeremy, who had stationed himself by the serving table and was acting as wine steward, intervened, "we have two, Henri and Pierre".

"Then please extend our congratulations, the food was superb" said Joe.

"Thank you sir, I will tell them. When you're through we will serve coffee in the main salon".

After the coffee had been served and the Brandy and other drinks offered, I asked Sandy to collect the balance of the crew together to meet our guests. Jeremy herded the two shy chefs ahead of him as if they were sheep going to the slaughter. As soon as they had been introduced they excused themselves and fled back to the galley.

Bima joined me on the aft deck, leaving his father in conversation with Jeremy, while Melanie and Jasmine compared earrings.

"I must admit that I'm surprised, I was not expecting such a show boat" he said with a complimentary air. "I honestly hope you can dispose of the stones, my father is enthralled with the yacht, and it will add years to his life if he can find an outlet for his energies".

"Where are the stones now?" I inquired.

"Here are the same six" he answered as he handed me the little black bag "the balance will be available to you in London in two days. We will arrange for you to collect them from our London office. I doubt that you would have wanted to carry them all through customs".

"Melanie will be glad" I commented.

"I like her very much" he stated emphatically "what are your intentions?"

"You sound like her father. In case you've forgotten I'm a married man, like you!"

"She's in love with you, you know?"

"I know." I replied sheepishly "she'll be hurt and that's the last thing I wanted for her. But she's known from the start that there was no future for us".

"Things can change" he muttered philosophically.

"One never knows" I added.

He stood by the rail and stared into the water for a while, I guessed that he was contemplating his own relationship, having similar thoughts to me, trying to balance the importance of family against fantasy. It has always been a judgment of mine that many men live in a world of fantasy. They may be in the real world in business, but when it comes to matters of love or lust, the realism goes out the window and is replaced with fantasy. That old expression that men never grow up, applies in spades to men like me, and most likely to Bima. But I wouldn't have it any other way! Are we pathetic? Maybe!

"Girls like Lyn are very different to girls like Melanie" I said quietly, "it's one of the differences between our cultures. Lyn will be proud to have been your mistress, a man of such high stature, you'll treat her well I'm sure, but you'll forget her and so will your wife. Oh yes, I'm sure she knows, but it's expected, a part of being your wife".

I paused for a moment but Bima chose not to say anything, so I carried on with my philosophical sermon.

"My wife will be just the opposite if she finds out, she'll curse me, try to ruin me and divorce me. Adultery in our culture is not permissible. Meanwhile the adulteress, Melanie in my case, who entered the relationship with complete knowledge of the facts will lobby for the divorce and expect to pick me up on the rebound. A calculated risk, based on men's' fantasies".

"You're quite cynical".

"You're right, but I know it's true in my case".

We wandered around the boat to the front deck carrying our drinks with us, Bima settled onto a deck box and reminisced "Do you remember the day we met?"

"At Ascot" I replied "it seems so long ago".

"What was it? Ten, twelve years ago, I was single then".

"And miserable as I recall".

"Not miserable, lonely. I had no friends then, I have very few now. I'm rich and will be richer one day, but so what, I have children, a wife who loves me, and yet…"

"You feel like your missing something" I interjected.

"Exactly. You feel the same?"

"I always have. I've had this conversation before, with myself. I'm scared because now I may know the answer. What's missing is not something tangible, and it's not someone; it's a deficiency from inside, a lack of belief maybe, or a self conscious awareness of your own vulnerability coupled with an inability to make a commitment. If you are like me then you never allow anyone to get close, not your wife, your kids, no one. And why is that? You're scared that someone will find that there's nothing inside, just a shallow excuse for a man! It's as if you're incomplete, a part is missing, and no one is able to fill the void except yourself, by accepting who you are and understanding that you're no different from anyone else. Nobody is perfect".

"That's rather frightening, but I readily admit that some of what you say is correct, but it's easier not to face the problem".

"For a while. It won't go away".

"What do you charge for these sessions?"

I laughed at his joke "Let's go join the others".

CHAPTER ELEVEN

Melanie still had an apartment in London that she had shared with another law student.

"It's nothing fancy" she had warned me "but it's convenient to the Underground".

"Are you sure that the other girl won't be there?"

"What girl are you referring to?"

"You said that you had a room mate?"

"And you assumed that it was a girl".

"Well, yes. I'm sorry, I had…"

"Loosen up David, I was teasing you" she smiled "it was a girl, but she's gone".

"I'm really up tight, I've never been so nervous. So close, I just know that there's a calamity waiting to happen".

She led the way to the second floor of what she called a masionette, to me it was a duplex, similar to one that I had rented myself when I had attended college.

"Home sweet home" she sighed, as she opened the door and carried her bags into the living room.

It was comfortable, off the beaten track and out of Charlie's scrutiny. I had checked for a tail at every opportunity during our departure from Bermuda and our arrival in London. I was sure that there was no one watching, and this flat would be impossible to trace. I was convinced that Charlie was lurking around the proverbial corner, he had to know that I would return to London, that I would come home to my family.

In just forty eight hours I would return home, because by then the money would be deposited in my account and out of reach. But for the next two days I would have to be extra cautious, and this apartment suited me just fine. When Melanie had mentioned that she still had a month left on her lease, I jumped at the chance to stay with her.

"I'll put the kettle on" I offered "we have to drink tea now that we're here in jolly old England".

"Take these" she said as she extracted the little bag of diamonds from her bag.

I had asked her to carry them through customs as I knew that I would be searched. It's one of the disadvantages of my line of work, that whenever I present my passport a red light flashes and I'm treated like an ex con, or a wanted criminal. The experience at Heathrow had been exactly as I had predicted, my bags were thoroughly searched and I had been asked a million questions about the reason for my trip, where had I visited, what had I purchased, how long I'd been away and on and on. They had finally passed me through and I had joined Melanie who had been waiting patiently for over an hour.

"What was that all about?" she had asked.

"Routine for me whenever I travel. I must be on a list of suspicious characters. It keeps me honest" I had joked.

The apartment had two bedrooms, both with twin beds; there was a small kitchen, a smaller bathroom and a living room. The furnishings were well worn but clean, to say that it was cozy would have been an over statement, adequate would be more appropriate. I hesitated at the bedroom door, undecided as to what our sleeping arrangements were to be.

"Push those beds together" called Melanie without hesitation, as she had observed my predicament, "it's too cold to sleep alone".

I did as she had suggested and wondered if that had been her normal routine when she had entertained. I felt a pang of jealousy, I was now in her environment and inserted into her bailiwick, this was where she existed, where she functioned, where she led her life before I had whisked her off to satisfy my fantasy.

"Is everything ok" she asked.

"I was day dreaming".

The kettle whistled for attention "I'll make the tea" I announced.

I knew relatively nothing about her. Yes, she was a lawyer and had completed a course in criminology, she lived on an island in the Bahamas, she had a brother, she could swim, play golf, dance and hold an intelligent conversation with a Prince. But that was all. I had no idea of what her aspirations might be; she had chosen to be a lawyer for a reason, a tough choice for anyone but much tougher for a girl from the Out Islands. Did she want kids? Where did she want to live?

"How's the tea comin'" she called from the bedroom, where she was busily unpacking her suitcases.

"What?"

"The tea?"

"It's just about ready, steeped to perfection".

"Were you dreamin' again? Is something wrong?"

I poured the tea and carried the cups into the bedroom.

She looked at the cups with a smile, "where's the milk, and the sugar? Your mind is off some place else".

I went back into the kitchen to find the sugar and the milk. I must have lingered too long because Melanie came to find them for herself. She sat down opposite me on one of the kitchen chairs, took my hand in hers and repeated her previous question, "what's wrong David? Talk to me, I want to help".

"It's this place" I stammered, "it's yours; it represents the life I know nothing about. I've been terribly selfish, dragging you around the world, not caring about you or your desires. Sitting here I realized that I know virtually nothing about you and in a couple of days I'm gonna just walk away".

"But I knew that at the start".

"It's so unfair. I want you to tell me all about yourself. I need to know the real you, where you're going, who with and what you want to achieve. I want all the pictures, not just the last one on the roll".

"Where do I start? Number one, you didn't drag me around, I came voluntarily and I had the best time of my life, it's an experience that I'll never forget, something to tell my grandchildren about someday. I had time on my hands, I'd finished my course here and was going home to decide whether I should become a practicing lawyer at home or venture out to the States or come back and practice in England. This experience has helped me make that decision, I'm going home to hang up my shingle, maybe I can help my own people in some way".

"I'm so happy to hear you say that. Is that why you chose to become a lawyer?"

"I was motivated by my father, and now I see the wisdom of his advice. He worked as a caretaker for an American family for a long time before they eventually sold their home and moved back to the United States. The man was a lawyer and my father realized the opportunities that came across a lawyer's desk had enormous potential for both the lawyer and his clients. He thought that it was essential that a Bahamian lawyer be involved in matters of concern to the Bahamas. As he often said 'For too long our affairs have been handled by foreigners'. They sacrificed to send me to school in Nassau and later here. It was the proudest day of their lives when I graduated. So I'm going back".

"And what about your personal life, husband, kids, all the usual things. Are they in the overall plan?"

"No, I like children, other peoples, but I'm not the mothering type. A husband would be fine, but it will take a very special man, and they just don't exist in the Islands".

"Where did you learn to play Golf?" I asked.

"In England, I had a friend that designed golf courses, an ex pro; he taught me how to play".

"No romance there".

"No, he was too old, close to sixty".

She was still holding my hand as she struggled to continue. I could sense that the words were caught in her throat as she looked directly into my eyes and said "I didn't expect to fall in love with you"

"I don't know what to say" I said weakly "I'm flattered, and under different circumstances I would be ecstatic, but you know I can't tell you that I love you".

"You can if you do?"

I thought of my conversation with Bima about the shallowness of men and their fantasies as I strived to find the right words and extricate myself from this confrontation.

"Whether I love you or not is irrelevant Melanie, surely you can see that?"

"You're avoiding the issue. It's a simple question that requires a simple answer, whatever the consequences. You can't qualify love".

"Spoken like a true attorney, direct and to the point" I chuckled "can I plead the fifth?"

"It doesn't apply in this case".

"Then my answer is, Yes, I do love you".

"The prosecution rests" she proclaimed.

"May I approach the bench?"

Without waiting for her reply I reached across the table and kissed her.

"One more question" I continued "is it permissible for the defendant to make love to the prosecutor?"

"You bet!" she yelled "just let me get out of these robes!"

I had forgotten how early the sun sets in England, it was barely five o'clock and yet it was dark outside. We had made wonderful tender love, the kind that's reserved for couples in love, and now I was both thirsty and hungry. I hated to break the romantic mood, but a man cannot live on love alone, my energy level was low and I needed refueling.

"I'm hungry" I said without an excuse for my interruption.

"Me too" she said "I'm starving".

"I fancy something simple for a change; my stomach can't handle anymore gourmet meals. Is there a pub close by?"

"The Rose and Crown is just a couple of blocks away"

"Is the food good?"

"For a pub, yes. I've eaten there a hundred times".

"Well, let's go".

I was excited about visiting a place that Melanie had frequented; there was a chance that I'd meet an old acquaintance of hers who could give me an insight into a different side of her. I felt a need to absorb her short life into mine, there was no ulterior motive, so common in my usual relationships, I just wanted to learn more about her. I have a closet full of secrets and she must have one or two.

After the phoniness of Las Vegas I was looking forward to being back in an English pub, where the customers were real, like the characters in Eastenders, and where the staff thrived on the bickering, the complaints and the continual banter between the regulars propped up at the bar and those who had to force their way through them to buy a drink.

Melanie had searched for a hat to wear before she had left the flat, she had finally located it perched on a set of golf clubs in the closet in the second bedroom, and now she wore it as we entered the pub. The hat was a golf cap with 'Titleist' embroidered on the front and with 'Champions' on the back.

I stood back to allow her to enter, as a gentleman should; within ten seconds I heard a whoop from the barman as he recognized her, followed by a chorus of voices chanting Tiger, Tiger. And as if from nowhere music started to play, it was an old song from the twenties called Tiger Rag, there was no refrain just the continual repetition of three words 'Hold that Tiger'. Every patron joined in echoing those three words as Melanie was twirled and dipsy- doodled around the floor, as partner after partner grabbed her for a short dance.

The bartender signaled to me.

"You with the Tiger?" he shouted above the noise.

I assumed that Melanie was the 'Tiger' so I answered in the affirmative.

"I've never heard her nickname before" I told him.

"Just look at her. Ever seen her play golf?"

"Yes I have, she beat the crap out of me".

"Well there you are mate; she's another Tiger Woods".

The music finally ended, Melanie escaped from her last admirer and joined me at the bar.

"Tiger eh?" I laughed, "if only they knew how the name really fits you".

"I played on the Pub golf team, and we were lucky enough to win. They all called me Tiger after that, and the name stuck. They used to play the music every time I came in".

"You're they're hero".

I had the feeling that I was the first 'date' that she had brought to the Pub, just about everyone in the bar came to shake my hand and to offer to buy me drink. A few warned me to make sure that I treated her right or I'd have them to contend with, most said I was a lucky 'son of a bitch' or some other equally endearing term, several were just plain happy to know that she had found a boyfriend.

Our complimentary drinks were lined up across the bar from one side to the other, I looked for someone to thank as I sipped my first English draft in a while.

"We came here to eat" Melanie told the bartender.

"The Tiger needs feeding!" he called out.

A table was cleared, scrubbed and dried, napkins were arranged and cutlery positioned and then we were escorted to our table.

"It's on the house" he informed us, as he transferred the drinks from the bar to our table.

It was clear that the opportunity to have a quiet talk with Melanie would have to wait until later. I wanted to relate to her the story of my encounter with the DeBeens family because I knew that she had been convinced by Bima, Jasmine and Joe that I really had no chance of disposing of the diamonds. I could tell from the not to subtle hints in her conversation on the subject that she didn't want me to be too disappointed if the Indonesian's predictions turned out to be true.

"I was just imagining the kind of reception you would have received if we had visited this place on Friday or Saturday, instead of a quiet weekday evening"

"The regulars are here everyday, and they are the ones who care" she said.

"I would have been embarrassed, but you handled it beautifully, I feel pretty lucky".

"Well thank you. I know they'd like to get to know you".

"Some other time, maybe tomorrow in fact. If all goes well I'll want to celebrate".

"It may be our last time together" she said sadly. "I want to be alone with you. Not here".

I was not looking forward to our 'last supper'. I knew that she would cry, and I might join her. Farewells are not my strong suit. I had been trying to find a way to avoid the inevitable, but so far had not been able to find a solution.

"Do you have a place in mind?"

"No, but it needs to be quiet and romantic, not a Pub".

"And after? I mean the next day?" I hesitated, unable to find any easy words, "when I'm gone".

"I'll fly home; maybe I'll meet an interesting man on the plane".

"Fat chance" I commented, "lightning doesn't strike twice".

"You're right, but let's not talk about the future, when today isn't ended. Live for the moment is my motto, and at this moment I couldn't be happier".

Melanie deserted me at the insistence of a group of her boisterous friends who intercepted her on her return from the ladies room. She threw her hands in the air in demonstration of surrender as she sent an apologetic smile in my direction. A gray haired man slipped into her vacated chair at our table.

"Mind if I join you?" he asked.

"Please do. You're a friend of Tigers?" I asked.

"I taught her to play golf. A natural, could be a pro if she wanted, like a daughter to me she is". He stopped to regain his composure before continuing "Sorry mate, my name's Bert".

We shook hands.

"I'm David. You did a great job. She's terrific".

"Very talented girl, pretty too, and kind, very kind."

"I know".

"She used to read to my wife, God rest her soul, before she passed away. She would come to the house almost every day and read to her. Books mostly, I don't read too well myself, so she came. Never asked for anything in return, used to make tea for her, sometimes she'd bring some cake or biscuits, and she'd read, for hours. Very kind she is. So I taught her to play, it was the only payment that she would accept".

I offered him one of the drinks that were still on the table. He downed a larger and continued.

"You gonna marry her?" he asked.

"Too early to tell" I answered.

"You'll never do any better. She's one in a million! Smart too, you know she's a lawyer? She helped a lotta people in these parts with legal advice, an' all for free. Wouldn't take a penny. They love her here".

"I can tell".

"Let me buy you a drink" Bert insisted.

"No, no thank you. There's still a back log at the bar, we can't possibly drink anymore. Here have another".

"I met her Mum and Dad when they came for her graduation, really nice people, you can see where she got it from, her looks I mean, her mother was a looker. From the Bahamas, an island somewhere, I've seen some pictures, looks too hot for me!"

Melanie extracted herself from her friends and rushed over to embrace Bert. They hugged for a while before she sat down.

"I bin talkin' to your fella".

"His name's David"

"I know. I was tellin' 'im as how you used to read to Ethel".

"She taught me a lot" said Melanie, 'she was a fine lady".

"You gonna marry this one?" he asked.

He has a fixation on marriage, I thought.

"He hasn't asked me yet, but I'm working on him" she responded with a smile. Melanie winked at me and stood up to leave.

"We have to go" she announced, "it's been a long day. We just arrived this morning and I'm weary".

We shook two hundred more hands, heard two hundred more sexual comments about what we might be doing later and why we had to leave so early, and left to a final rousing chorus of 'Hold That Tiger'.

We walked the two blocks to the apartment arm in arm, neither of us wanted to be the first to speak. We were both deep in thought, replaying the events of the evening and knowing full well that our time together was dwindling. Melanie was the first to speak.

"What time is your appointment tomorrow?"

"I'm to be at Consolidated at ten. Then the big one is at eleven".

"You're cutting it close, aren't you?"

"The two buildings are practically next door".

"Will you tell me why you're so sure that you can sell them?"

"I plan to tonight, in bed".

"Before or afterwards?"

"Before, and if you don't fall asleep or die from boredom, there will be an afterwards, I promise. It's a long story".

We undressed quickly and snuggled under the covers in an attempt to keep warm. It's cold in England!

She rested her head on my chest and said "I'm ready, don't make it too long".

"I'll start in the middle of the story, by telling you that this all occurred six years ago in Botswana. I was in nearby Namibia working as a consultant to the Police Department. A series of robberies had been committed that all included a safe cracking episode and since that's where my expertise lies, they called me in to help with the investigation.

Debeens Diamond Mining Company operates more than twenty mines in South Africa, Tanzania, Botswana and Namibia, they are one of the largest employers in these countries and they contribute a major share to the economies of those countries. DeBeens is a family controlled empire, Dutch in heritage and almost two hundred years old. In their early days they supplied their own law and order in the form of a large well trained security force, whose ruthlessness is legendary in this area. Their practices have been mollified but there still exists an animosity among many of the miners, and rebelliousness is not uncommon.

Six years ago a group of rebels entered a mine office in Botswana, shot three of the office workers, kidnapped the plant manager and blew up the vault. The plant manager at that time was Eric Debeens, the grandson of Frederik DeBeens the head of the company, its largest shareholder and now the Chairman of the Board. The rebels were not looking for diamonds, but cash and the incriminating police records of their compatriots. The office was surrounded by police, but a standoff existed because of the boy, he was nineteen at the time and being groomed to become the Managing Director."

"But you weren't there?"

"That's right, I was Namibia, and had no idea what was happening. But the rebels had bungled the job on the safe, as most amateurs would; they had blasted the mechanism so badly, that even with the combination, the safe could not be opened."

"Ah, ah, David to the rescue".

"Exactly, I was the expert, even the rebels knew of my reputation and they agreed to let me open the safe. The Police flew me by helicopter to the mine to assist. When I arrived, I could see that it was an ugly situation, tension was high and tempers were close to boiling over. There was a huge crowd of angry mine workers booing the police, who were unable to remove the bodies of the dead or offer any real solution to the situation. As the helicopter landed I was accosted by old man Frederik himself, he pleaded with me to try to save his grandson, and to give the rebels anything they wanted. The head of the security force briefed me; he said that there were three rebels inside, all heavily armed, and their captive Erik Debeens. The rebels also had a supply of plastic explosive and had agreed to let me enter, providing that I was unarmed."

"You must have been scared to death".

"I was terrified, but I had told them that I would help. I needed some supplies. I needed detonators, more explosive, anti detonation head phones but no weapons. I knew that I'd be searched and that these men were desperate. With my hands over my head I slowly walked into the mine office. There were four, not three dead employees, three wild looking rebels and their prisoner. He was close to death, his hands and feet were tied much too tightly and he was trussed up like a chicken from behind. I knew that my priority was to get him untied. I took one look at the vault and determined immediately that it could not be opened. Not by me or anyone else. It had been blasted out of shape. I was desperately formulating a plan to convince the rebels that I could open it. I took a small mallet from my bag of supplies, donned a pair of headphones and began tapping the outside of the vault."

"What were you trying to find?"

"Nothing, I was playing a game. Trying to convince them that I knew what I was doing. After a while I stopped my tapping and withdrew a plastic sheet from the bag and taped it across the door. I made a series of notations on the sheet that I hoped the rebels would think corresponded to the placement of the explosive charges. They watched intently as I went through my process of subterfuge. When I had finished, I stood and demanded that they untie Erik.

They refused. I packed my bag and walked towards the door to leave. They grabbed me and dragged me back, but they knew that they couldn't force me to open the vault. The chief rebel walked over to me with a knife, I thought he was going to kill me, but instead he cut the ropes on Erik. They allowed me to help him into a chair, he was in dire condition but at least he was alive and would remain so if my plan worked."

"You had time to work out a plan?"

"It was simple. In a confined space such as the office, a major explosion would burst a persons eardrums with such force that their brains would implode, killing them instantly. I had sufficient explosive to produce such an explosion. Very carefully I worked the plastic explosive around the top and sides of the door to the vault; I wanted them to believe that I was preparing to open it. I explained to them that it would require three simultaneous charges, two from the right and one from the top. I set the charges and ran four wires; I gave each one of the rebels a detonation switch, while I had the fourth. Unknown to them only my switch was connected. I put anti- detonation headgear on Erik, and handed the same gear to the rebels. I had to, if I hadn't, they'd have been suspicious. The trick would be to get them to remove their head gear and leave their ears exposed to the blast. I rehearsed them to push their switches on the count of three. I whispered to Erik, told him to make sure that his ears were always covered. My one hope was that as soon as the police heard the explosion they would come running. We were ready. I counted to three. One, Two, and Three. The rebels pushed their switches and as I had planned, nothing happened. Two of the rebels threw off their headgear and rushed to check their wires. I made the connection with my switch and hurled myself to cover Erik. The blast killed the two rebels instantly, while the third was thrown twenty feet across the room, he landed in a heap against the far wall, but he recovered quickly and started firing just as the police entered. They shot him. They carried Erik and me outside to a waiting ambulance. Frederic Debeens traveled with us to the hospital, speaking in Dutch to his precious grandson for the entire journey. I had been hit in the leg by a bullet, and the force of the explosion had given us both a pounding against the office wall, but we would recover.

Frederik came into our small hospital room to watch as the doctors and nurses tended to our wounds, he looked directly at me with tears in his eyes, he took my hand from the white hospital sheet, held it to his heart, and said very quietly but with conviction 'I can never repay you for what you did today, but if ever you need anything, no matter what the cost, come to me and it will be yours. I am in your debt for ever!'

I never saw him again but I came to know his grandson Erik very well, we are good friends".

"What a story"

"And that's why I know that he'll buy the stones from me tomorrow".

"He has to. I was wrong to have had any doubts".

"The story was meticulously concealed from the press and the media, Debeens went to great lengths to dispel any rumors that came to light, they were afraid that the news would spark riots in some of their other mines. So there was no way that Joe or Bima could have known of my connection to the DeBeens family, nor of their obligation to me".

"Do you have an appointment with them?"

"Tomorrow at eleven. I called Erik to let him know that I was in town and that I wanted to discuss some business with his grandfather. I never mentioned payback time! They're expecting me in the morning".

"You must be excited, but you're not showing it? I feel excited for you".

"I know that I won't sleep much tonight. I hope I don't keep you awake".

"I doubt that I'll sleep either, I have a few decisions of my own to wrestle with".

"We both need the rest after such an eventful day, but if sleep is going to elude us, I have a suggestion".

"I'm all ears?"

"Just cuddle up here, in bed together, no sex, no teasing, I just want to hold you, asleep or awake. I want to feel the warmth of your body and the closeness of your heart. I feel vulnerable for some reason, and I need your love".

"I love you so much, David. I don't know how I'm going to get through the day tomorrow knowing that I may never see you again".

I could feel her tremble against me and the wetness of her tears on my chest, as she melded herself into the contours of my body. I dozed for a while, then woke again; she was still crying quietly in her sleep. I had never expected to feel this way about any one, a mixture of love, concern, shame and disgust. I really had become a rotten bastard, and to top it all off I had sucked a wonderful young girl into my web of deceit, lies and theft. It should be easy for me to rationalize our situation and conclude that she was over twenty one and able to take care of herself, or that she knew what she was getting into, or that she would learn from the experience and be wiser and smarter in the future. I guess I do have a conscience, because no amount of rationalization could dispel the burden of guilt that I felt. But what could I do? To promise her that I might find a way for us to be together, would just compound the problem, and be a promise that I knew that I couldn't fulfill. It would be a last futile attempt to appease my guilt, the kind of promise you would expect from a scoundrel like me!

I cannot remember the last time that I cried, but lying in bed that night with Melanie, holding her so close that I could feel her heart beating and her whimpering, as the tears formed again in her eyes, I wept with her.

CHAPTER TWELVE

The offices of Consolidated Mining were located on High Holborn East, just a short walk from Hatton Garden where the London Diamond Exchange was located. My appointment was for ten o'clock.

I had traveled to the City by Tube, the local name for the underground rail system which traverses London and many of its suburbs; I had walked to the Turnpike Lane station from the apartment, caught a train to the Holborn station and then walked to Consolidated's office. I had a letter of introduction from Joe, but I was sure that I was expected. I was ushered into a modern suite of offices by an attractive Indonesian receptionist. The offices were in stark contrast to the exterior of the building which dated back to the sixteenth century. After a considerable show of bowing and scraping by an office flunky, who had taken the place of the receptionist, I was escorted into the office of the London manager.

I identified myself, and was about to show Joe's letter, but it was waved aside by the manager. A small safe built into a wall cabinet was secretly opened and two velvet bags were removed and placed on a well lighted table in front of me. He handed me a magnifying glass and said that he would return in thirty minutes.

I emptied the bags onto the black table top, adjusted the overhead light, and examined the diamonds. There were four hundred and ninety four of them, all of the same high quality, I could find nothing wrong with any of them, the colour, cut and clarity were like the six I had in my pocket. Joe and Bima had fulfilled their part of the deal, it was now up to me to reciprocate.

The manager returned in exactly thirty minutes, he checked to make sure that I was finished, he watched me as I placed the two bags of stones in my briefcase, then he led me back to the flunky, who in turn escorted me to the reception area and out onto the street. The whole process had taken less than an hour.

I wondered if any of the pedestrians that I passed could tell that I was carrying 125 million dollars worth of diamonds in my briefcase. I took an apprehensive look at each passer by as I walked to the head office of DeBeens. Their office was located on Holborn Viaduct in a section of the city that dated back to Roman times, and to where the origins of many of the old buildings could still be traced.

Here I was greeted by a Dutch receptionist, then shown into Erik's private office.

Erik Debeens had grown up in the past six years, he was heavier around the middle, his hair was thinning and his face was creased with worry lines.

"David, my friend. What a pleasure" he said, as he slapped me across the back and put his arm around my shoulders, "you're a sight for sore eyes".

"How are you?" I asked.

"Never better, and you?"

"Still struggling along" I joked.

"Grandfather is looking forward to seeing you. He often asks after you".

"How's he doing?"

"Still as sharp as a tack, he keeps us all in line".

"Then let's go see him".

We walked through the central office pool, where a dozen girls were busily working at their computers, then up a flight of stairs to the executive floor. At the far end was the office of the Chairman of the Board.

Erik rapped on the door and we entered. Frederik looked the same as he did the last time that I had seen him in the hospital in Botswana.

He rose slowly from his desk chair and came to greet me. He seemed genuinely pleased to see me once again; he ordered coffee for us all and invited me to sit. When the coffee had been served he came directly to the point.

"Something tells me that this is not a social visit" he said.

"No it isn't" I replied.

I had rehearsed my opening little speech over and over again while I had lain awake last night, trying to find a subtle way to inform him that I was here to collect on his promise. He surmised from my hesitation that I was having a difficult time trying to find the words.

He waited, just as I would have done if our roles had been reversed.

"I have a business deal for you" I started out by saying, "I want you to buy what I have in this briefcase. Not because I want to take advantage of you, but because it is a good deal for both of us".

I took the little bag from my pocket and handed it to him. He held one of the stones under his desk lamp and examined the stone with his jeweler's eye glass.

"Very nice" he commented, "Erik, take a look. "Are they hot?"

"No sir, they're quite legitimate, I have the necessary warrants. They are from the Kalimantan region".

"You want to sell them? Right?"

"Yes, and not to some discounter who could upset your market".

"Six little stones wouldn't upset the market" he scoffed.

"I have five hundred of them in this briefcase".

There was a brief silence in the office following my announcement.

Erik was the first to speak.

"Can we see them?"

I opened the briefcase and removed the two bags of stones. Erik cleared a space on his grandfather's desk and spread the diamonds out for their inspection. Frederik phoned for an appraiser to come to his office. A short bespectacled man hobbled into the office, and was directed by his boss to evaluate the stones.

"He'll take an hour or so" said Frederik, "will you join us for luncheon?"

He saw my look of anxiety, "we won't steal them" he reassured me.

"But will you buy them" I asked calmly.

"David my boy, I made you a promise six years ago. I would like to honor my debt to you before I pass on".

I felt a wave of relief surge through my body. All that was left now was the price.

We walked out into the sunshine, down a narrow passage way, under an arch, that had a sign above it for the Mitre Pub and into Ely Place.

Off to the left was St. Ethelred's church, and it was here that we were to have lunch. I followed my hosts down into the crypt where a busy crowd of blue suited clones was eating. We found a table and settled down.

"You were born here, in London, David?" he asked.

"Yes, not that far from here".

"I'll guarantee that you never knew that this place existed. Ely Place is not a part of the City of London. It's like the Vatican is to Rome and is under the jurisdiction of the crown. This church dates back to 1293 and this crypt predates that and there is also a part of a Roman Basilica here".

"And who operates this café?"

"The vicar of the church".

"He must be Dutch" I joked.

"He's German actually" he laughed.

The conversation during lunch continued on in a light hearted manner, no mention of our afternoon's business was made. I guessed that, 'no business during lunch' was a policy that the old man insisted upon. He told me that after my release from the hospital in Botswana, the vault that had been the object of the whole incident had been removed with a heavy crane to a safe location where it was painstakingly taken apart. It took many men several months, and had cost a fortune. When it was finally opened, they found that it contained less than three thousand dollars in cash, no diamonds and none of the police records that the rebels had been after.

"To think we nearly died for three thousand bucks" Erik commented.

Back at the Chairman's office, the appraiser had completed his job and left a report on Frederik's desk. I was given a copy as we made ourselves comfortable for an afternoon of haggling.

"How much do you expect to receive?"

I looked him in the eye and without hesitation said, "fifteen thousand a carat".

"I'm not going to haggle with you David, but fifteen is too high. It is not our usual policy to buy cut stones from outside sources, but I will make an exception in this case. As you are no doubt aware it is impossible for a diamond to be traced to it origins after it has been cut, so no one will know where these came from. I'll give you twelve".

"I'll take it" I answered immediately.

We shook hands, and I turned to shake hands with Erik.

"Where would you like to be paid?" he asked.

"Would you wire the money to my Swiss account?" I asked as I handed Erik a copy of the wiring instructions and my account details.

"I'll take care of it immediately" he said as he left the office, leaving me alone with Frederik.

"David, I don't want to know the circumstances under which you came into the possession of these stones. They are quite unique and very beautiful, but you must understand that the market for stones of this quality is extremely limited; we may have to wait several years to sell them all. I'm glad that you had the foresight to bring them to me, we would have been very unhappy if these stones had been allowed to upset our market. I hope you're satisfied with our offer?"

"I'm happy" I commented, "more than happy, and you can rest assured that I will not ask you for another favor. We're even!"

Erik returned carrying a wire confirmation advice notice.

"The money is on its way. It should be in your account within the hour, here's a copy of the transit information for you".

He handed me the paper, and I placed it in my empty briefcase. There was nothing more to say, our business was completed and it was time for me to leave. We shook hands, said our goodbyes and I departed.

I walked quickly to the first Pub I could find on Holborn Street and ordered a large drink. My hands were shaking as I sipped from the glass. I'd done it! My life would never be the same.

I extracted my copy of the appraiser's report from my pocket and reread his findings; the only part that I was interesting in was his final calculation of the weight of the stones. He had reported a total weight of eleven hundred and sixteen carats, and at a price of twelve thousand dollars a carat, the amount of the wire transfer was just a few dollars short of thirteen and a half million.

I made the phone call to the lawyer in Bermuda, and told him to release the yacht's papers to Joe.

I was anxious to get back to the apartment to share the news with Melanie, but I couldn't arrive empty handed. I found a taxi and asked the driver to make a couple of stops along the way. First stop was to buy Champagne, second stop to buy flowers and the third stop was at a dress shop that had a white cocktail dress in its window that Melanie had drooled over every time she had passed. The taxi stopped outside the flat and while I fumbled for the key, the driver unloaded my packages onto the curb. I carried my purchases inside as I called out that I was home. I sounded something like Fred Flintstone.

There was no response to my calls, she was not there. I hoped that she hadn't gone to the dress store to buy the white dress. Her absence provided me with the opportunity to hide the dress, arrange the flowers and set the champagne on ice, before she returned.

I looked in the kitchen for a suitable vase for the flowers and saw a note propped against the salt shaker on the kitchen table.

Dear David,

I received a phone call from my brother earlier, my father has suffered a major heart attack, I am catching a plane home immediately. Hope all went well, I don't know if I will ever see you again. Love Melanie.

I collapsed onto a kitchen chair. My mind was racing in a hundred different directions. Could I catch her at the airport? Should I telephone her home in Harbour Island for more details on her father's condition? Was there some way that I could help? Should I fly to Nassau?

She was GONE!

I was devastated by the note. I was overcome by compassion for her and I had some understanding of the trauma that she must be experiencing at this very moment on her journey home. Our last night together had been last night, and our plans for tonight's celebration would never take place. I buried my head in my hands and remained immobile at the kitchen table while I contemplated my options.

There was only one, and it was the one that I had known that I would have to make from the start. I had to go home. Home to Laura and Annie. I had to put Melanie out of my mind and return to my normal life.

I packed my bags once again and prepared to leave the flat. There were still lots of Melanie's clothes in the closets and I knew that it would be necessary for her to return after the funeral to collect her things. I hung the new white dress beside her few other dresses and pinned a note on one of its thin straps, it read:-

'Think of me when you wear this. All my love, David'.

I replaced the flowers in their box, discarded the little card on which I had written a cute note to Melanie, and after ensuring that all the windows were secure, I closed the front door of the apartment and this episode in my life.

It was ironic to arrive home and make the same Fred Flintstone announcement "I'm home!"

Nobody came running to greet me, there was no wife or daughter with their arms spread open to hug me and welcome me home. The house was quiet. I dropped my bags onto the floor and called once again "I'm home! Is anyone here?"

I heard a door open upstairs and a mumble of voices, at least someone was home. But it wasn't Annie or Laura that shuffled down the stairs. It was Charlie! He was zipping his pants and tucking in his shirt, and just a step behind him was Laura struggling to pull a house coat around her.

"You son of a bitch" I yelled, as I rushed up the stairs to beat the daylights out of him.

"Calm down David" screamed Laura. "It's over!"

"You bet it is" I shrieked.

I was at a disadvantage being at the bottom of the stairs, Charlie was able to ward off my blows by kicking at me, but I did manage to grab one of his legs and drag him down to ground level. I punched him a few times, but found myself being pulled from behind by Laura.

"I'll kill you, you two timing bastard" I yelled.

It was over in a few minutes, I couldn't fight both of them and I had no desire to hurt Laura. It was clear that they both were ready to kick me out of my own home, and there was not much I could do to prevent them.

Laura threw a set of photographs at me, they were pictures of Melanie and me in Harbour Island, at the Hoover Dam and in the Grand Canyon, most were innocent, but two of them showed us kissing in more than a friendly manner

"I've always suspected, but never could prove anything" she hissed. "I never knew you preferred dark meat!"

"Your man took these?" I accused Charlie "I thought he was tailing me for the money?"

"I don't want your money. Laura is the best thing that ever happened to you, and you couldn't see it, you had to screw around. She's the only thing of yours that I want".

"Who is this tramp?" demanded Laura.

"She's a Bahamian girl, she's no tramp".

"And where is she now? Back home with a few dollars in her pocket for her services?"

"Where's Annie?" I asked, "does she know what's going on?"

"She's at Karen's, I'm sure she knows something".

"So you're planning to shack up with this piece of crap?" I motioned to Charlie.

"He loves me!"

"Oh sure he does now, but for how long? The only person Charlie loves; is Charlie. You have no idea what you're letting yourself in for. I know him better than you'll ever know him and I've seen him in action, he's had more women than you've had hot dinners!"

We argued and screamed for another hour, but I knew the situation had been resolved before I had returned. Laura wanted to be rid of me, she had the goods on me, and as my lawyer friend would have said 'case closed'.

Charlie had plenty of money so restitution was not an issue, neither was alimony or child support, they just wanted to see me gone. Did I have a choice? No.

My only concern was Annie. I asked Laura to allow Annie to call me, and to let her visit me if she wanted.

"Where will you go?"

I knew exactly where I would go, but I answered "To a hotel, then I'll decide. I'll let you know".

"I'll send your stuff".

"Thanks" I mumbled.

It was not as hard as I would have imagined to just walk away from my wife, friend and lover of nineteen years, and from the house we had struggled to buy when we were first married.

The house had been Laura's choice; I had told her that we couldn't afford the price that the agent was asking but she had managed to persuade the owner to carry a second mortgage for five years, so we had moved in. We had no money for furniture; we had covered the windows with bed sheets and slept under itchy blankets on a bed that we had borrowed from her parents. Three years later, when Annie was born, we had borrowed money from the local bank to buy baby furniture and to decorate one of the bedrooms as a nursery. Laura never complained about the hard times or the sacrifices she was forced to make, because of my inability to hold down a regular job or by my frequent absences.

I had grown to like the house and its compact garden, I had built a garage, an ornamental fish pond and several rose arbors. Our neighbors had become our friends over the years, and it was this sense of belonging that I knew I would miss.

I told the taxi driver to stop at Karen's house.

"Wait for me" I told him.

I could here loud pop music coming from the house, which gave me the hope that Annie was inside.

I banged on the door and yelled for her. I saw her face in one of the upper windows as she looked out to see who was at the door.

"Dad" she shrieked "You're home. When did you arrive?"

I finally received a welcome home hug.

"I just got here".

"You've been home?" she asked hesitantly.

"Yes. Charlie was there with Mum. It looks like I've been kicked out".

"He gives me the creeps" she shuddered.

"What do you mean?"

"He watches me all the time, like he owns me".

"Mum says he loves her".

"Mum's lost it Dad. This creep has bamboozled her; he's convinced her that you're a lost cause".

"She wants a divorce and I'm not gonna fight her".

"But what about me?"

"That's why I'm here. I want you to know that I love you very much and as I see the situation, you have three options, staying with Mum and Charlie, or coming with me, or going to college".

"Where are you going to live?"

"I don't know yet, but I have quite a lot of money in the bank, please don't tell your mother, and I can live just about anywhere I choose".

"If I go to college, you're saying that I could stay with you between semesters?"

"You've got it; I'll fly you anywhere you want and as often as you want".

"Is there a girl, Dad?"

"Yes. What have you been told?"

"Charlie said that you were 'shacked up' with a nigger".

"I met a girl on the plane on my way to the Bahamas; she's a Bahamian, a bright and intelligent young lady. She's a lawyer, and yes she has dark skin, darker than yours or mine but not pitch black like the African slaves you see in the movies, she's more olive coloured. She looks like Halle Berry".

"She's pretty then?"

"Charlie thought so when he met her, his exact words were 'she's a knock out', but that's beside the point. She's in love with me, and I love her".

"I've never heard you say that before".

"I've never been able to, until now".

"How old is she?"

"Twenty eight, you'll love her, she's fun to be with".

"I'm looking forward to it. Will you phone me and let me know where you are?"

"You can count on it, and you have my mobile number, it will reach me anywhere in the world, and I can call you back".

"I think I'll find a good college Dad, I like that idea".

"A very grown up decision, one you won't regret. I'm very proud of you. I just wish that I could have been a better father to you".

She hugged me and said "It's tough being a father to a brash teenager, Dad; you've done a fine job. Now I've got to go. Call me!"

The taxi took me back to Melanie's flat.

During the ride I had thought about Charlie and his motivation for seducing my wife. He had always kidded me about my good fortune with the girls when we had grown up together; I always went home with the good looking ones, while Charlie was usually stuck with the homely ones. When I had met Laura, she was with her girlfriend and I was with Charlie. The four of us double dated a few times, simple visits to the movies or the local disco; there had never been any friction between us or any jealousy, that I had been aware of. Had Charlie always harboured a desire to be with Laura? Had he been waiting for me to destroy my relationship for all these years?

Charlie had never married anyone, I used to kid him that he was too picky, once I even suggested that he was gay, it was meant as a joke but he didn't see it that way. Could he have been in love with Laura from that first meeting? In many ways I hoped that he was, it was reassuring to know that at least he would treat her right.

The fact that Charlie knew about the bank robbery in Spanish Wells should have been a major concern to me, but it's a strange circumstance that scoundrels, like me and Charlie, have a mutual trust of each other, no matter what conflict may exist in our personal relationship. In this matter I was confident that I could trust him.

No matter how hard I tried to make Charlie appear as the bad guy in this marital mess, I couldn't divert the blame; I was the culprit, the guilty party, the adulterer and the home breaker. It was all my fault and just like every criminal my main regret was not the crime, but the fact that I had been caught!

How could I possible pursue Melanie, knowing that I was incapable of sustaining a relationship, after all I had professed to have loved Laura. Yet I still messed around!

I would remember this day for the rest of my life for its highs and lows. In the morning I had become a millionaire, in the afternoon I had lost my girlfriend, and then I had lost my wife to my best friend, then I had been evicted from my home, but later I had entered into a better relationship with my daughter. It was enough to drive a man to drink!

But since I didn't have a car to drive, I walked to the Rose and Crown.

"On your own?" asked the bartender.

"'Fraid so".

"No Tiger?"

"She flew home; her Dad had a heart attack".

"I'm sorry to hear that. He was here once, seemed like a nice enough fella".

"Yes, I know. Bert said that he came for his daughter's graduation".

"How come you didn't go with her? I thought you two were a couple?"

"I had some business to do this morning, she left me a note".

"Well, when you talk to her, be sure you send my condolences".

I moved from the bar to an empty table to avoid an inquisition. I didn't have the answer to the question of why I was here while Melanie was home in the Bahamas. Normal couples share their feelings, their thoughts and opinions, their dreams, simple conversations and confidences; we had not reached that level. We had come close but I was guilty of erecting a wall around me, to restrict any access, to keep the one person that I loved from getting too close. It was a repeat of the pattern that had haunted me all of my life.

Bert walked in; he saw me alone at my table and came to join me. We exchanged 'hello's', he asked about Tiger, and I told him the news and answered the same questions that I had been asked by the bartender. I bought a round of drinks and sat staring into my glass.

"What's wrong?" he asked.

"You don't want to know" I replied.

"Try me, talking about a problem can help".

I hardly knew this man, but maybe that was a good thing, and I know he thought the world of Melanie, so I proceeded to tell him some of the story that had resulted in our meeting and subsequently to her departure earlier this morning. I never mentioned the money, for obvious reasons, but I confided in him about the doubts that I had concerning my suitability as a potential partner for Melanie.

"I could tell from the body language she exhibited the other evening that she loved you" he said.

"And I love her" I added.

"But you don't think that that's enough?"

"It's not that simple. We started out as friends, both prepared to have a good time, and then move on. It became serious sometime later; we both knew there was no future. I'm married, or I was until today, my wife wants a divorce".

"Sounds perfect! What's the real problem?"

"I'm a lousy partner, unfaithful, a woman chaser, not the sort of person you would want for Melanie, for God's sake. I'm not the sort of person *I* would want for her. I'm not good enough, she deserves someone better!"

"She should be the judge of that".

"Maybe, but I'm not so sure. You see, our whole relationship began on the wrong track; I was in the middle of a major scam and sucked her along. Oh sure, she knew and took her chances, but it hangs over us like the Sword of Damocles. I just can't start a serious relationship with this hanging over me".

"Then straighten it out first".

Bert had hit the nail on the head. Without the burden of the robbery on my conscience and the potential danger that I had created for Melanie, I might be able to quell the uneasy feelings that I had been having about us. Would I have any hesitation in chasing after her if I had not stolen the money? Was it the knowledge that she possessed that made me feel inferior? Did I want her to think better of me?

I had confessed 'on the witness stand' that I loved her without qualification, but I knew that it was unrealistic to love someone blindly. Melanie may hold the belief that love is blind, but from my limited experience it was clear to me that love is based on trust and for her to trust me knowing that I was a scoundrel and a thief was asking too much.

There was no way that I could rectify my years as a scoundrel but if I could return the money to the bank it might restore my reputation.

"Let's have another drink, Bert. I think that there might be a solution".

"I hope so, for her sake".

From the very moment that I had robbed the Royal Bank, I had experienced a feeling of remorse. It had nagged at me on every occasion that I was alone, and it was becoming an irritant. Remorse is a word that is not normally in my vocabulary, especially for an institution like a bank. In fact it wasn't the bank; it was the people of Spanish Wells whose lives I may have effected that bothered me. I knew that individually none of them had suffered any loss, but the Island itself must have lost a piece of its untarnished reputation as a crime free place. If I could somehow return the money and make the whole episode appear like a gigantic prank, then Spanish Wells could once again hold its communal head high. A noble gesture, but how could I bring it of?

The Bank's prime interest would be in getting its money back, and from the scant information that I had gathered, there was some evidence that they thought that the robbery was most likely the work of some local person or group, who had the money and was having a hard time getting rid of it. After all who could they suspect? There were no clues, no sign of any elaborate escape and no evidence that the money had left the Island. For all they knew, it could be hidden on one of the smack boats, or buried in the rubble by the bridge to Russell Island.

"You brain is working overtime" Bert commented. He had been looking for a sign that I was ready to continue our conversation "This round is on me".

"Keep 'em coming, a few beers will help me to face this challenge" I said, "and believe me, this is quite a challenge".

"I'd like to help?"

"I have to do this myself; I need to sleep on it".

"Well, when you're sleeping on it, make sure you spend some time dreamin' about Melanie".

"You can be sure that I will. I dream about her even when I'm not sleeping. She's in my thoughts all the time".

"Will you call her?"

"In a few days. Right now I think I should let her deal with her family problem, give her a little space".

"You're wrong" Bert said emphatically "she needs to hear from you".

"Ok, I'll call her when I get home or first thing in the morning".

"Now, drink up and get out of here" he urged.

By the time I reached the apartment it was almost ten o'clock. I had reached a decision while I had been walking and could hardly wait to make the phone call. Maybe she would be in bed but as Bert had so rightfully pointed out, Melanie needed to hear from me.

The phone rang eight times before it was answered. I asked if I could speak to Melanie, and after what seemed like a long wait I heard her voice.

"How are you?" I asked "I hope I'm not calling too late? How is your father?"

I had to ask the question about his condition, even if the answer would be difficult for her talk about.

"Hi David" she whispered, "thank you for calling. Dad had passed away by the time I arrived home, the funeral is tomorrow".

"I'm sorry. I would have liked to have met him. The fellas at the Pub send their condolences. How are you holding together, and your Mum? How is she?"

"We're fine, sad but fine. All the family is here so she has plenty of support. Tell me how did your meeting go?"

"It was a piece of cake" I answered.

She laughed over the phone, probably her first laugh for a couple of days.

"I miss you" she said quietly, "do you miss me?"

"You know that I do. I'm staying at the flat, I hope that's Ok?"

"Of course it is. I'm flying back right after the funeral".

"Let me know the flight. I'll meet you at the airport".

"There's only one flight, the day after tomorrow. I'll look for you, now I must go. Someone wants to use the phone. I love you David".

I told the dead phone that I loved her, she'd already hung up.

My next call was to Annie.

"Annie its Dad"

"Hi Dad, what a surprise".

"You said I was to call you, so I'm calling. Any news?"

"From the home front? No, Mum agrees that college is a great idea, in fact I'm thinking about making the trip to Bristol tomorrow to check it out".

"Want some company?"

"You mean it?"

"Sure, I'd love to come with you. I'll rent a car and pick you up at nine. How does that sound?"

"But your car is in the garage."

"It was my car. I don't want to borrow it. I'll see you in the morning".

I slept like a baby. A clear conscience and the seed of an idea germinating in my brain helped me to sleep, for I knew that in the morning the seed would have already put down roots and be on the way to blossoming. I Called Executive Car Rentals and asked them to send over a sports car while I busied myself around the flat. Fifteen minutes later a driver rapped on the door with a set of keys in his hand, I signed the required papers that had been filled out by his office, as he waited impatiently by the front door.

"It's the red one down the street" he said "I couldn't find a spot any closer. Drive carefully and enjoy. See ya!"

His mate was in another car waiting to drive him back.

I collected my mobile phone from the charger, made sure that I had cash and credit cards in my pocket, locked the front door and went to meet Annie.

The red car was a Jaguar Convertible with only fifteen hundred miles on the odometer. It was a warm morning so I pushed a button to put the top down, put her in gear and took of like a bat out of hell! I honked outside my old house hoping that either Laura or Charlie would catch a glimpse of the flashy car, but they were probably still in bed because the only person I saw was Annie as she came running out of the house with a flabbergasted look on her face.

"Dad, are we going in that?"

"Sure, do you like it?"

"Its gorgeous" she stammered as she touched one of the fenders.

"Here" I called, as I threw her the keys "You drive!"

"Are you sure?"

"It's not mine! Its rented, if you're comfortable with it, then so am I"

"Are you kidding? It's what every blonde Bimbo dreams about" she laughed. "Hold on tight. Here we go!"

As we drove westwards out of London on the M4 motorway Annie talked about her reasons for wanting to attend The University of the West of England. I had known for some time that she had an interest in medicine; she had been enthusiastic about learning to be a veterinarian when she was thirteen, and later on was equally as keen on being a midwife.

She explained that her real interest was in diseases, particularly those that effected children in the poorer countries of the world. UWE taught a four year B.Sc. Honors course in Biomedical Science, and Annie wanted to learn more about it.

She proceeded to quote statistics to me that proved that more people died each day from curable diseases than died in traffic accidents. She explained that the life expectancy in many African countries was less than forty five years, and that each year saw a rise in deaths due to lack of treatment facilities and insufficient money.

"Aids alone" she said "will kill more people next year than the total number of people that died in all the world wars combined. Its just shocking, Dad"

There was nothing I could say, except to encourage her and express my support for her choice.

"I think you can make a difference. My generation has been oblivious to the problems, but yours can effect some changes that may save mankind, or make this world a more equitable place to live in".

"I hope I can contribute in some way. I don't expect to find the cure for cancer or any other such disease, but there are hundreds of ways that biomedical research can increase the world's knowledge of Applied Genetics, Genomes and other technologies".

"You've made up your mind that this is what you want to do?" I commented.

"I've given the subject a lot of thought, I'm passionate about contributing and this University course fits the bill".

"I'm overwhelmed, but proud to hear what you intend to do. So many people have these great noble intentions but do nothing about them. I hope you stick to your goal".

"I will, you can count on it".

We continued on our way to Bristol at record speed in the red Jaguar. I had never ridden in a convertible before that I could remember, and never on a Motorway, it was not my favorite mode of transport. It was noisy, dusty, windy, hot and inconvenient.

Annie must have been having a similar reaction to the ride because she pulled off the road and proceeded to put the roof back up.

"I hope you don't mind?" she said.

"I've been trying to find a way to suggest that you put the top up ever since we reached the Motorway, but I thought you would think I was being an old fuddy-duddy".

"Dad, that's one thing that you aren't, for a father you're pretty cool".

"I'm actually blushing" I joked.

"Oh Dad!" she exclaimed.

She asked me to check the road map and to look for the exit to Bristol.

We left the M4 and slowed down to a safe speed on a narrow country road for the final few miles to the City of Bristol. I suggested that we stop for lunch before we reached the University.

"Your choice" I said "I'll eat anything!"

Anything but fast food, I thought, but declined to say it.

Annie stopped at quaint little cottage that had a sign hanging from a wrought iron doorway that proclaimed that luncheon was being served.

"Is this Ok?"

I was already out of the door as I said, "something smells good".

If we had searched all of South Western England we could never have found a restaurant to equal this tiny establishment that Annie had stumbled upon. If there had been six star rating instead of five, it would have been awarded all six. The menu was almost as thick as the Bristol telephone directory, with a selection of dishes that were both unusual and tempting. The wine list was also something to behold and featured wines that even to my limited knowledge were virtually priceless.

"You hit the jackpot, Annie".

"It's expensive!" she exclaimed as she perused the menu.

"If I order a bottle of wine, will you have some?"

"Just one glass, I'm driving".

I ordered a bottle of Lafitte Burgundy from the extensive wine list, and for lunch I ordered Tournedos Rossini, while Annie selected the Dover Sole Amandine.

It had been a long time since I had spent such an enjoyable time with my daughter. It was from a combination of circumstances that we had an unusual relationship, yet right at this moment in these surroundings we both felt closer than we had for a several years. Maybe we had both grown up!

"Do you know what your plans are, Dad?" she inquired.

"I haven't got the complete picture yet, but I have an overall plan in mind, it's the details that aren't pinned down".

"Is it a secret?"

"No, but I do want to talk to Melanie about it, 'cause it includes her".

"Melanie is the Bahamian lawyer?" Annie asked.

"Her father's funeral is today, and tomorrow she's arriving here. I'm planning to meet her at the airport".

"In the red Jag?"

"I guess so. I've been staying at her flat near Turnpike Lane, but I'm thinking of buying a house in Spanish Wells and moving to the Bahamas".

"Does she know?"

"Not yet, I plan to talk to her tomorrow when she arrives here. She told me once that she wants to practice law in the Bahamas, so that means that she's going home. I thought it would be nice if I was close by".

"And you like Spanish Wells?

"I know that I was only there for a couple of weeks, but there's something about the place that appeals to me. The people are great, there's no crime, very little traffic, and you can get almost anything you may need. It's civilized and easy to fit in. I really like the place".

"But what will you do, Dad? You're too young to retire".

"I can fish. I may write a book and I just might return to my first love and compose music, or I could be a private eye for Melanie's law firm, there'll be plenty to keep me occupied".

"And I can visit you?"

"I'm counting on it".

"I'd like to meet Melanie when she's here?"

"That'll be wonderful, I know you'll like her, and she'll love you".

As we exited the restaurant we were asked by a man who I assumed was the owner, how we had enjoyed our lunch. I told him that everything was excellent and that I would certainly be back for dinner very soon. I was thinking of bringing Melanie here. He

217

responded by suggesting that I make a reservation for some time in the future as they were completely reserved for the next four months, in fact, he said, there was a long waiting list of customers who hoped that a reservation would be cancelled. When I asked him about lunch and the fact that we had arrived by chance, he told us that opening for lunch was a new experiment and that this was their first week of the new schedule, he went on to say that the reservations were beginning to come in thick and fast as his clientele was becoming aware of the new time table.

We spent the afternoon exploring the Frenchay Campus of the University. Annie wanted to visit the laboratories that specialized in biochemistry, histology and hematology; she also wanted to chat with some of the senior students who were in their final year of the course. I was very impressed with her knowledge and with the penetrating questions that she asked. She walked me through the Students Union section, where she collected an armful of pamphlets about every conceivable facet of the University. She checked the campus faculty area to talk to two Doctors that she had had some previous contact with, and then we spent a few minutes looking at the dorms, the cafeteria and the library. She was finally finished.

Annie asked me to drive home while she digested the information that she had collected. I welcomed the silence as it gave me the opportunity to gather my jumbled thoughts together and to try to put them in some order. The events of the last two days had left me slightly numbed, and I wanted to be sure in my own mind that I knew what I wanted, before I confronted Melanie with the news. I had conceived a devious plan to return the money to the bank, a plan that I would have to share with Melanie because I would need her assistance. I was also apprehensive about her reaction to the news that my wife wanted a divorce. Would she automatically assume that I had deliberately instigated the idea, and presume that she was to be my new partner?

Did I want her as my new partner? I just couldn't say the word wife.

I convinced myself that the best course of action was to take it slowly, and let events happen in their own time. Don't rush into anything. What is that old saying about 'out of the frying pan into the fire'?

"I'll spring for an apartment off campus if you'd prefer it to living in a dorm" I announced.

"Dad, it'll be too expensive. But thanks. It would be nice".

"I told you before I have the money. Think about it, I want you to be happy; a happy student is a successful student. I'll throw in a new car as well!"

She leaned over and hugged me, almost causing me to swerve into the adjoining lane.

"You can't be serious" she exclaimed "can you really afford it?"

"Can you keep a secret?" I asked, and then continued on without waiting for an answer "I have more than five million in a bank in Switzerland collecting interest. The interest alone will buy you a new car!"

"Mum doesn't know?"

"No, it all happened while I was away. I was planning on telling her when I came home, but Charlie changed all that. You do know that Charlie is worth a fortune? So she won't need anything from me".

"I don't want anything from him" she stated.

"Then let me be the generous father. We'll all go car shopping tomorrow or the next day".

"I don't know what to say Dad, except thank you so much".

"I'm tickled to death to be able to do it. Now where do you want to be dropped off?"

"I have to stop at Karen's to tell her all the news".

Karen was on the front doorstep when I pulled to a stop in front of her house. She did a double take as she saw Annie climbing out of the passenger seat. Her hands went to her mouth to stifle the scream as she came running to the car to hug Annie and to gape at the red Jag.

"Oh my God" was about all she could say, and she repeated the same three word phrase over and over.

Annie leaned in and planted a big kiss on my cheek as she thanked me once again. I told her that I would call her to go shopping for the car after I had collected Melanie. I stepped on the gas and went back to the flat.

CHAPTER THIRTEEN

The British Airways flight from Nassau departed at six in the evening which meant that it would arrive at Heathrow at seven the next morning. I estimated that it would take Melanie an hour to deplane, to clear customs and immigration and to be ready to be picked up. In spite of my calculations I still arrived an hour too early, and that was after I had wasted an hour having an early breakfast just to pass the time. I hadn't been this excited for a long time.

I kept reminding myself that she had just buried her father the previous day, and that I would have to contain my joyful enthusiasm until I had had a chance to gauge her mood. I checked the arrivals board once again to confirm that the flight was on time, and then took my place outside the International flight arrivals door along with ten thousand other excited waitees.

Slowly, one by one the passengers came through the doors to yells from waiting family members. There was no doubt that this was the correct flight as it was easy to distinguish these folks as Bahamians.

And there she was, walking proudly through the line of waiting kinfolk, scanning the crowd and looking for a friendly face.

"Melanie" I yelled "Over here!"

If I had any concerns about her frame of mind, they were dispelled immediately as she dropped her bags and practically threw herself into my waiting arms.

221

Our embrace and the kisses that followed was not just the normal greeting that you would expect from even a close relation, but was that of two estranged lovers, reunited after an emotional parting.

"Oh David" she sobbed "I missed you so much. I couldn't wait any longer to come back here. Please take me home and make love to me?"

And I did!

We stayed in bed most of the day, we made love, we slept, we sent out for a pizza that we consumed in bed between our love makings, we showered together and made love again.

She recounted the sequence of events that had taken place after she had received the phone call from her brother telling her of her father's heart attack.

"I had to leave immediately. I tried calling you on your mobile, but I couldn't make contact with you. I didn't know how to reach you, I was frantic".

"I'd turned my phone off. I didn't want to be disturbed during my meetings. I'm sorry".

"I wasn't sure that I would see you again. The possibility of never seeing you again made the grief for my father even more intense. I cried on and off for two days. Your phone call came at the perfect time, I was able to get a hold of myself and start to feel positive again".

"It was Bert that insisted that I call, I wasn't sure that you'd have wanted me to intrude. I'm glad I did".

"I'm glad too. By the time the funeral was underway I'd cried all my tears away and exhausted all my grief. There were more than two hundred people at the ceremony, many who had known my father all his life, they came to support my mother and to offer their help. They came from all over the Bahamas, from Spanish Wells, Gregory Town and Nassau, many of them distant relatives that I had never met before".

"How will your family survive, financially?"

"Mother has her job, and my brother lives at home. They'll be all right. Now tell me your news!"

I started at the beginning by telling her how I had visited Consolidated's office and collected the diamonds without any hitches.

"I felt euphoric as I walked the few blocks to DeBeens, just knowing that I had millions of dollars worth of diamonds in my briefcase. While one of their appraisers evaluated the stones we went to lunch in the crypt of an old church that doubled as a restaurant. It was a weird scenario and I don't remember much about the place or what we talked about during lunch. Back in the office I was handed a copy of the appraiser's report, it was standard jargon verifying the colour and clarity, the one detail that pleased me was his finding that the total weight was eleven hundred and sixteen carats; more than I had calculated and more than Joe had told me. I asked the old man for fifteen thousand per carat without blinking an eye, but I can tell you that I was nervous, my stomach was in knots! He waited for a moment before he answered, it was the longest moment of my life, and then he said very calmly that fifteen was too high and that he'd only pay twelve. I accepted right away, I'd already done the math, I knew the exact amount".

"And did they give you a check?"

"No, the full amount was wired directly to my Swiss account, I waited in their office for the confirmation and then I left".

"How much was it?"

"Twelve thousand dollars times eleven hundred and sixteen carats comes to exactly thirteen million, three hundred and ninety two thousand dollars!"

"Oh David, that's a fortune".

"I know, but don't forget I have to deduct the legal fees"

"What fees?"

"Yours of course. You did all the paperwork for the 'Princess'" I said as I extracted a check from my pocket and handed it to her. "Here's a check for fifty thousand; I would like to make it more but I know that you'll fight me about it"

"David, I can't accept this. It's too much".

"Don't be silly; fifty thousand is fair for a transaction of eight million. Now don't argue" I insisted.

"You're very generous. Thank you. What happened next?"

"As you could imagine I was on a high, I wanted to celebrate; I wanted to share my good fortune with you. I bought some champagne, a bouquet of flowers and that cute white dress you'd been drooling over…"

"The one in the window? You bought it for me?"

"It's in your closet" I said.

Melanie jumped out of bed, naked as the day she was born, threw open the closet doors, found the dress and pulled it on over her head.

"It's beautiful David. What do you think?" she asked as she twirled around the bed.

"It's perfect. You look terrific, but underwear would help cover the dark patch at the front" I laughed.

She threw the pillows at me, jumped on the bed and began to pummel me with her fists as she giggled with uninhibited pleasure. I gave in to her onslaught, caught her fists and pulled her close. She relaxed and kissed me with a mixture of passion and gentility as I carefully checked out the stitching from the inside of her dress.

"Is the Champagne in the fridge?" she asked as she carefully removed the dress and returned it to her closet. "And what happened to the bouquet?"

"When I found your note I was devastated; I toyed with the idea of following you, but decided that I shouldn't intrude into your family's tragedy. I wandered around the apartment for a while, finally deciding that I had to go home to my wife and daughter".

"You gave my bouquet to your wife?" she asked accusingly.

"Yes" I replied "I thought it might soften her up, but I was wrong, she threw it at me".

"Why?"

"I found my old friend Charlie there. While you and I were cavorting around the world, Charlie had maneuvered himself into my wife's bed. He had a stack of pictures of the two of us, some in compromising positions that his sleuths had taken. He wasn't after the money; he was after evidence of my unfaithfulness".

"But he's your best friend?"

"He was" I stated "anyway the result is that my wife wants a divorce, and I can't fight them, even if I wanted to".

"It's all my fault David, I'm so sorry. I feel terrible about this".

"No one's to blame, least of all you. It was my doing; I just got caught this time".

"What will you do?"

"I have a plan, or at least the seed of a plan. I think you know how I feel about you, and I want you to understand that I want us to be together, but our relationship has been built on a slippery foundation. I'm referring to the bank heist. I have to put the money back, turn over a new leaf, start a new way of life in order to earn your trust".

"You know that I trust you, and I love you just the way you are. But if you feel that you have to do this for yourself, then I'll help you, if I can. I liked the part about us being together" she added with a smile.

"When you were back in Harbour Island did you hear any mention of the bank robbery?" I asked "And you mentioned that there were family members from Spanish Wells at the funeral, did the bank ever come up in their conversation?"

"Never, it's like it never happened".

"There has to be a reason. My guess is that because the money was all in Bahamian dollars which are virtually worthless outside of the Bahamas, the bank officials are convinced that the money is still in the country somewhere, and they are waiting for the thief to show his hand in some way. If that is the case, then they are really only concerned with the return of the money".

"Are you serious about giving the money back?"

"I'd still have almost five and a half million. We can live on that!"

"You said 'we', what does that mean?"

This was the crux to the whole relationship. 'We' to any girl implies marriage, kids, family and commitment, whereas to a man 'we' has many alternate meanings, such as living together with a commitment, or living together without a commitment or living separately as boyfriend and girlfriend. I had backed myself into a corner. It was time to fish or cut bait!

"The 'we' means us, you and me together. Finding out more about each other, learning to respect and trust each other, listening and advising, caring and needing, and understanding who we both are and where we want to go in life. It will take time but I'm ready to start".

"Sounds like a proposal to me" she said.

"Yes and no" I explained "I'm still married at this moment, but I believe that we need time to get to know one another, after all we only met three weeks ago and under peculiar circumstances".

"I agree with some of what you said, but I'm going home in the next few days, as soon as I pack my books and things".

"I know, I'm going with you!" I announced.

"To Harbour Island?"

"Possibly, I had thought of buying a house in Spanish Wells, in fact I think a law practice in Spanish Wells would do well. You might consider hanging your shingle there".

"Let me get this straight. Are you planning to live in the Bahamas? Or just spend a few weeks there on vacation?"

"Maybe I wasn't clear in my choice of words. I want to be with you in the Bahamas! If you are going to live there, then so am I! My only qualification is that I think that I would prefer Spanish Wells over Harbour Island, but I could be persuaded otherwise. For a law practice I really think that Spanish Wells offers the best opportunity. You could operate in both places quite easily".

"I'm thrilled David naturally, but are you sure?"

"Unless you have a hidden sinister side, or you turn into a vampire at the full moon, I'm willing to take the risk. I can't imagine living anywhere without you. You bring out the best in me, you make me happy about myself, and for the first time in my life, I feel that I'm complete, whole, fulfilled and that that elusive missing ingredient has been found".

She rolled her body on top of me, took my hands in hers and stretched them to the top corners of the bed, then her feet intermeshed with mine and she forced them into the bottom corners so we were spread eagled together, face to face with every part of our two bodies touching.

I could feel her heart beating, her chest rising and falling and her breasts throbbing as she covered my mouth with hers in long seductive kiss.

"This all of me" she whispered "what you feel is what you get. Now turn over".

We reversed our positions with me on top as we spread ourselves out and reached for the four corners of the bed with our hands and feet. It was one of the most sensual experiences I had ever had.

"This exercise removes your vulnerability" she explained, "it's natural to want to curl up in a fetal position, to be secure. Stretching is the reverse and it makes you feel exposed, almost as if you've sacrificed yourself to me and me to you. It's what you've been missing, the freedom of just being yourself without the need to protect yourself or to feel that you need to conceal any part of your body or your soul".

She was absolutely correct, I felt totally exposed but completely comfortable, and for once I was an open book and relishing the new experience.

"Thank you Doctor Freud" I joked.

"Now that I have you relaxed and on top of me, I want to ask you something?"

"Go ahead".

"Could you please move; you're heavy?" she laughed.

I adjusted my position and moved my dead weight from her by sinking a few inches lower in the bed. Our bodies were still in total contact but now with different segments aligned. It occurred to me that who ever had designed our bodies should have won some prestigious award, for he or she had excelled in their profession.

I told Melanie about the offer that I had made to Annie, and asked her if she would like to go car shopping with us. I called Annie to tell her that we would pick her up at ten the following morning. She asked if Karen could tag along, and it was agreed that we would meet them both at Karen's house.

Annie had decided that she wanted a Toyota Camray.

The dealer was dumbstruck when we drove into his parking lot in the red Jaguar convertible; he was totally blown away when three attractive girls emerged from the car. I explained to him that Annie was my daughter and it was she who would be choosing the car, Karen I explained was her girlfriend and Melanie's role was never defined. He knew that she wasn't Annie's mother, but he never went there.

Having a common interest such as choosing a car was the catalyst that brought Annie and Melanie together. Fortunately for me, Annie had determined the exact model that she wanted so the only minor detail left open for discussion was the selection of the colour.

Choosing the colour took an hour and I shuddered to think how long we might have been at the dealership if Annie had been undecided on the vehicle's other specifications.

She finally settled on something the salesman referred to as teal; it looked like pale green to me, but I didn't say a word. All that remained was the price and I stepped forward to play my masculine role of knowledgeable buyer and negotiator. I took Annie's hand in mine and walked with her to the office. Melanie intervened, she grabbed Annie's arm from me and told me, in polite terms, to get lost. I threw up my hands and let two girls take over.

Fifteen minutes later Annie beckoned for me to come into the office, my presence was required to write the check.

"Toughest negotiator I've ever met" commented the salesman. "She should be working for the Teamster's Union".

Evidently Melanie had scrutinized the purchase contract, picked a few holes in the ambiguous language, rewritten part of the service contract and beaten the price down to such a low level that even the sales manager had to excuse himself from the negotiations because he felt faint.

"She was terrific Dad" exclaimed Annie when we were all back in the Jag. "They didn't know what had hit them; she even talked them into giving me an extra six months on the warranty, plus a freebee when mine's in for service. Thanks Melanie and thank you Dad!"

"Where did you learn so much?" asked Karen.

"I studied contract law in my final year of law school" answered Melanie.

"You're a lawyer?" asked Karen in disbelief, "I'm sorry I didn't mean anything by that, I had no idea. You're pretty cool".

"It's Ok. I'm used to people not expecting me to have a brain".

"Me too" I commented, "but in my case they were usually right. I'm glad I'm good at one thing though".

"What's that?" they asked in unison.

"Writing checks and buying lunch" I answered "I'm hungry".

"That's two things" Melanie said.

"I stand corrected, counselor! Where shall we eat?"

Annie and Karen wanted to eat at The Greenery, a vegetarian establishment for the weight conscious. I was out voted.

While Melanie was washing her hands, Annie told me that she thought that Melanie was really terrific.

"She's smart, and fun and so pretty. I can see why you love her".

"I'm a lucky man" I commented, just as Melanie rejoined us.

"Why are you a lucky man?" she asked.

"Because I found you; and because I just found a fiver on the floor" I said, as I picked a five pound note from under the table. I don't think that my slight of hand fooled any of them.

Over lunch Melanie quizzed Annie about her decision to study Biomedicine, it was clear that she had more than just a working knowledge of the subject, and she asked several probing questions that Annie had to think about before answering.

"I think you're making the right decision and for the right reasons" Melanie commented after she had heard Annie's responses to her questions.

"Having a worthwhile career is vital for today's woman, not only does it establish our independence but it fulfills us and makes us more desirable and attractive. Gone are the days of our mother's generation, when all we were expected to do was stay home and have babies and clean up after the man of the house".

"But I want to have babies and stay home and clean up for my husband" said Karen.

It was Annie that answered.

"Staying home and having babies is fine, just be sure that you find a husband that will help you, not one who expects you to be his slave. I hope to have babies some day too; after all I want my Dad to be a Grandfather".

I looked at Melanie across the table, we made eye contact and I could guess what was in her thoughts.

"What do you think, Grandma?" I joked.

"Do you want children" Annie asked.

"No" Melanie answered, "For me the sacrifice is too great, and I'm not much on motherhood".

"Plus her boy friend has had a vasectomy!" I added.

"You have a boy friend?" asked Karen innocently.

There was a moments silence before she realized what she had said, then we all laughed at her remark together.

I offered to take Annie to collect her new car in the morning but she said that she could easily catch a bus.

"It's not far Dad. When are you leaving?"

"In a couple of days. Melanie has to pack her things, then she has to collect her diploma from school. I have to sign some papers for your mother's lawyer, and then we are on our way".

"What diploma?"

"I finished a course in criminology, its no big deal" said Melanie.

"Sounds like a big deal to me. I hope it comes in useful one day" I said.

I performed my bill paying function as expected and escorted the three ladies to the door. I drove back to Karen's house where the two girls said goodbye and left us to ourselves.

"Annie is a bright girl. She must take after her mother" Melanie quipped.

"Yes she does. Would you like to meet her?" I asked.

"Some other time, I'm going to be busy this afternoon" she said seductively.

"Doing what? Watching a movie? Packing?"

"I'm going to make love to you when we get home. And then we are going out to have a belated celebration".

"Just remember I'm going to be a Grandfather soon, take it easy on me".

"I'll be gentle old timer" she giggled.

"What exactly are we celebrating tonight?" I inquired.

"I'm glad that you asked. First, I have fifty thousand dollars in the bank, that's the most money I've ever had. Secondly you have thirteen and half million in yours, and I'm sure that's the most you've ever had and thirdly, you're getting a divorce and you sorta proposed to me. Are those enough reasons?"

"But I'm giving back eight" I said.

"I'm curious as to how you're planning to return the money to the bank without getting caught?"

"I'll tell you later. I don't want you worrying your pretty head about it; you've got more important things to do".

"Well let's get started!"

Our celebration started with dinner at Charo's of Duke Street, a small intimate place that I had heard of but had never been to. It was super, and exactly the right setting for Melanie to show off her new white dress. The small dance floor could only accommodate five or six couples, which made dancing very close an absolute necessity. We made an attractive couple and were totally oblivious to the other patrons in the room. I could have looked at Melanie for ever. She was exciting to be with when she was in such an attentive mood, she made me feel like I was a very special person and not the cheap scoundrel that I knew that I really was.

We danced until midnight, and then went home to bed. We were both tired after a strenuous day and were looking forward to returning to the Islands for a rest.

CHAPTER FOURTEEN

It was imperative that I make a visit to my bank in Switzerland. I had to ascertain the correct method of transferring funds from my account without leaving any trace. I had a fairly good handle on the type of transaction that would achieve the desired result, but I wanted to be sure.

I had made a reservation with the airline for a flight to Zurich that departed within an hour of Melanie's scheduled flight to Nassau. This would enable us to leave the apartment together and travel to Heathrow in the same taxi. There was no reason for Melanie to accompany me to Zurich, in fact I had told her that I only expecting to be there for a few hours to complete my business and then I would catch the first flight to Nassau. Rather than wait for me in Nassau it was agreed that she would continue on to Harbour Island and I would meet her there sometime later.

Annie had volunteered to drive us to the airport in her new car when I had phoned her to say goodbye.

"It's the least I can do" she had said "and I want to say goodbye in person to both of you. It may be a while before I see you again".

Melanie went to collect her diploma while I sought out the divorce lawyer. I had decided to use my usual lawyer to represent me, he was a friend to Laura and me, but was not representing Laura. Evidently Charlie had offered her the use of one of his many attorneys. After an hour of consultation I instructed my lawyer to allow the divorce to proceed as quickly as possible with no objections from my side, unless Laura had a change of heart about the disposition of our joint estate. I also changed my will to eliminate Laura. This action seemed to be a tangible end to our nineteen years of marriage. Annie would remain as my sole beneficiary, until I changed it again to include Melanie. In a fit of guilt I telephoned Laura from my lawyer's office.

"I called to say goodbye" I said sheepishly.

Laura didn't answer for a while, so I continued, "I hope that you'll be happy with Charlie, and that he'll treat you better than I did".

"I'll never forgive you, David. But for Annie's sake we must remain on amicable terms. She'll keep me informed about you. So it's goodbye", she said with finality.

"Goodbye Laura" I said.

I hung up the phone and thought how calmly we had just expunged the nineteen years of our lives that we had spent together. I wondered what the next nineteen years would bring. I was a much different person now to the naïve young man who had swept Laura off her feet. In my own mind I think that I'm a better person now, maybe a little less tolerant, but more considerate and less self centered. I understood only to well, that a life with Melanie would be wrought with challenges, some obvious and some not so obvious. Could our love overcome these challenges? Or were we both fooling ourselves for thinking that it would? In a few hours I would be embarking on a journey that would bring a radical change to my lifestyle with an Island girl, who was from a place that was light years away from my city dwelling beginnings. Would I be like a fish out of water, or was I mature enough to adapt to a different way of life? Only time would tell.

Melanie's flight was to leave at eleven and mine at noon. Annie arrived at the apartment at eight the next morning and helped us load Melanie's boxes of books and clothes into the trunk of the Camray. We had skipped breakfast to give us time to be ready for Annie's arrival. Neither of us was hungry, but I couldn't stop drinking. I finished off the milk, drank two cups of tea, a glass of water, yet still I was thirsty. Annie told me that she wasn't stopping for a bathroom break on the way to the airport, so I'd better be prepared to hold it!

We insisted that Annie drop us at the departures entrance rather than attempt to find a parking spot. This arrangement also made the farewells easier and shorter. We hugged and kissed, promised to phone regularly and threatened her if she failed to visit at her first opportunity. Then she was gone.

Melanie's flight was boarding as she clung to me and kissed me over and over again.

"I'll miss you" she cried.

"I'll be there as soon as I can. No more than a couple of days. I promise".

"Call me, when you have time".

"I will. I love you".

"Love you too" she said; and then she was gone.

A real unmitigated scoundrel, like Charlie for example, would assess my current situation and make, for him, an easy decision. Keep all the money, forget about the girl, live the good life on the Riviera or any place in the world and never look back. It was tempting and I gave the idea some consideration, but I'm not Charlie and I realized that I'm not as much of a scoundrel as I thought I was. The difference is that I do have a conscience and a trace of honour in me somewhere.

I boarded the Swissair flight to Zurich, happy in the knowledge that I just might be a decent fella with a future, if my plan to return the money to the Bahamian bank could be accomplished.

My telephone call to Laura had given her a jolt. She had not expected to hear from me directly and had been comfortable knowing that her lawyer presented a buffer between us that permitted her to deny my existence and the emotional tumult that I had brought into her life. Her emotions had been held in check ever since her spontaneous outburst on the day of my return and she had not allowed herself to dwell on the break up of the marriage or the termination of a relationship that for all it's heart aches had sustained her through nineteen years of her life. She could never forgive me for what I had done and she knew that the decision to proceed with a quick divorce was the correct course of action, but it was no so easy to wipe all the memories from her mind.

She had slipped into a relationship with Charlie far more easily than she would have thought herself capable of and she questioned the reason for her actions and found that she didn't care for the answer. Charlie had been available in her darkest moments, and he had been a shoulder to cry on and a pillar to lean against. She knew that she didn't love him, in fact as their relationship had progressed, she found that she was looking for excuses to spend less time with him rather than more.

Her relationship with Annie had become a major problem. Whenever Charlie slept in her and David's bed, in her and David's bedroom, she was overcome with feelings of guilt, and she had difficulty facing her daughter at breakfast on those mornings when Charlie was still there. Charlie's presence in the house disturbed Annie and she made no secret of the fact that she despised the man. Laura had to admit that his long association with the porno industry and its seedy characters embarrassed her and made both she and her daughter uncomfortable in their own home.

"Your father called yesterday" Laura informed her daughter.

"For me?" she asked.

"No. He called to say goodbye to me" Laura admitted.

"Well, that was nice of him. What else did he have to say?"

"He said that he hoped that I'd be happy with Charlie and that he hoped that Charlie would be a better husband than he had been".

"Mum, you're not considering marriage to this man. Are you?"

"No, I don't love him. He's just a good friend".

As Charlie descended the stairs, Annie excused herself from the breakfast table and disappeared into the back yard.

"Good morning Annie" he called to her as she left.

She never answered.

"She needs to change her attitude" he growled, "the little bitch"

"Don't you call my daughter a bitch Charlie. This is her home, and you make her uncomfortable here".

"I'll be glad when she moves out".

"I won't. I'll miss her".

"She'll be fine at college. Don't worry".

"David bought her a new car and he's told her to find a nice apartment off campus. I wonder where he found the money?"

"He robbed a bank!"

"Don't joke Charlie".

"He did. In the Bahamas. The stupid fool never realized that he'd wind up with a suitcase full of Bahamian dollars" Charlie laughed.

"When was this?"

"A couple of weeks ago, before he went to Vegas with his bimbo".

"I can't believe it. I've been so naïve all these years. He's turned out to be as bad as you!"

"Now hold on a minute. All that's in the past".

"Not from what I've heard Charlie. You're still up to your neck in porn, and you know it! At least David is only a thief!"

"And an adulterer, and a nigger lover".

"Annie liked her" interrupted Laura.

"She would of course" Charlie commented.

"What's that supposed to mean?"

"She'll say just about anything to contradict me. I know that she hates me. I can't wait for her to leave".

Laura listened to Charlie ranting on about her daughter's behavior and her bad attitude until she had heard more than she could stand.

"I think it's best if you leave" she said calmly.

Charlie pleaded with Laura for her to allow him to stay. He promised to try to befriend Annie and not be so critical of her. But he didn't know Laura like I knew her. When her mind was made up, there was nothing anyone could do or say to make her reconsider her decision.

Charlie was history.

I had made an appointment with Mr. George Bernstein of the Guardian Investment Bank for ten o'clock the following morning, he had recommended that I stay close to the bank at the Hotel Savoy En Ville. The hotel was located right on Paradeplatz in the center of the city. The taxi ride from the airport was only about a fifteen minute journey along Bahnhofstrasse through the outskirts of the city and to the hotel. I had reserved a single suite, an extravagance that I afforded myself in my new role as millionaire. The hotel was strategically located within walking distance of the banking district and just a short distance from the waterfront of Zurichsee. After checking into my suite, I went for a stroll through the old city. I sought out a jeweler whose name had been given to me by Bima. I had his address penciled on my golf score card from our match in Las Vegas, and over just this brief time it had become almost illegible. I found the establishment tucked between a bakery and a florist shop, the name above the door said Schubert's and as I entered a bell jingled in a back room somewhere, alerting the owner to the fact that he had a customer. From the look of the place I figured that he didn't have very many. The jeweler was not old, or German, as I had surmised from the name, but Asian. Most probably Indonesian, I thought.

I withdrew a velvet bag from my pocket and extracted a 'Sheekato' diamond. This one stone had mysteriously found its way into my pocket after the Debeens appraiser had finished his calculations. I could imagine the frantic counting and recounting that they had gone through to try to account for the missing stone. I'm sure that old man Frederik had blown a fuse and made all his staffs lives' miserable for quite a while.

I placed the stone on the counter in front of the jeweler for his scrutiny. He raised his eyebrows in approval as he examined the gleaming stone.

"This is the size" I said as I handed him a ring that Annie had loaned to me. She and Melanie had been trying on rings during their visit together and she had unobtrusively determined the size of Melanie's finger for me. "I need it by tomorrow".

"It'll be ready by noon" he told me. "Is this an Indonesian stone?"

"Yes it is. From Kalimantan; Bima Sheekato recommended you; I am a friend of his" I explained.

"Ah" was his only comment as he nodded his head up and down.

"I'll be back tomorrow" I said as I turned to leave.

I walked the few blocks to the waterfront and watched the activity on the water. Rows and rows of small boats were moored together in tightly packed numbers; most were small power boats that I assumed were used for weekend cruising trips by the local people. I compared the waters of the Zurichsee to those of the Bahamas, and thought that these people would go bananas if they were given the opportunity to cruise in their warm clear waters, instead of the murky cold water that they were accustomed to here. Nobody paid any attention to me and nobody waved or showed any sign of friendliness towards me, they all seemed preoccupied with their own importance and sought to keep themselves private. Their attitude provided reinforcement to my decision to live in the Bahamas where the people were open and friendly even to strangers like me.

I walked back to the hotel and spent a lonely evening by myself. The few patrons in the bar were unfriendly and coupled with the language difference it made the prospect of conversation additionally difficult. I had dinner in the Orsisni restaurant by myself and went to bed early. I was lonely and I was missing Melanie more than I would have expected.

Mr. Bernstein resembled a character that had been cast by a non- imaginative casting director to play the role of a bank manager in a low budget movie. He was dressed immaculately in a three piece dark gray suit; his white stiff collared shirt looked uncomfortable around his thick neck, while his maroon tie and matching hanky added only a trace of colour to his somber appearance. He insisted on addressing me as Mister David, a custom that annoyed me, and he placed the emphasis on the Mister rather than on the David, but I rationalized that I wasn't here to become his friend, so we proceeded with the business at hand.

I explained to him that I needed to transfer eight million dollars to an account in the Bahamas without the recipient having any knowledge of either the source of the funds or the identity of the sender. I had previously determined that a wire transfer to the Royal Bank had to clear through the Chase Manhattan Bank of New York, who would in turn pass the funds to the Royal Bank's operation center in Nassau; they would then route the funds to the specific branch and account number.

He assured me that the only information that would be available to the recipient of the funds would be the country of origin and the name of the Bank. There was no way that my name or account number could ever be traced.

"Secrecy is the core of our whole banking system" he stated, "however I will need the name and number of the account to which the money is to be transferred".

"I don't have that information with me. Can I advise you by telephone in a few days? Is that permissible?" I asked.

"We will need voice identity verification".

He saw the puzzled expression on my face and said, "come with me, Mister David".

I followed him into a sterile computer room where a lady technician was busily tapping on the keys of her computer. Mister George asked me to read my name, account number and password into a microphone that was attached to one of the computers. After a few moments the computer screen sent an acknowledging signal and played back what sounded like a tape of my voice along with a coloured graphical voice pattern picture.

"That's it" he said, "when you call the bank with the information, just respond to the questions that are asked and the computer will make the verification. It's full proof!"

"I'm impressed" I said with enthusiasm.

"It's the latest technology and is more reliable than finger prints. Are there any other matters that we can help you with Mister David?"

I thanked him for his assistance, shook his hand and exited the bank

I felt exhilarated with the knowledge that transferring the funds could be achieved without any risk to me. My plan was one step further towards completion. I had one stop to make in Zurich before I left.

I arrived at the little jewelry shop at ten minutes before my noon appointment. As I pushed open the door to the jingle of the warning bell and waited for someone to appear, I wondered for a moment if the jeweler had taken off with my diamond as I was sure that the stone was worth more than the contents of his entire store. My fears were dispelled when he parted the curtains that separated his small workshop from the front of the shop, and smiled at me from across the counter. He placed the ring onto a small black velvet cushion, and switched on an overhead light. He handed me his glass and motioned for me to examine the setting.

He had created a masterpiece. The intricate but uncluttered setting magnified the brilliance of the stone and did nothing to distract the eye from the stone's unmatched cut and colour. I turned the beautiful ring in my fingers to study every side. It was the most incredible piece of jewelry that I have ever seen. I was sure that Melanie would like it.

After complimenting the Indonesian craftsman on his outstanding creation, I made a promise to him to show the ring to Bima at some time in the future. I placed the little ring box in my pocket, paid him without any fuss or negotiation and then walked the few blocks back to the Savoy En Ville hotel.

None of the airlines that serviced the Zurich airport offered a direct flight to Nassau, which meant that I would have to fly to New York or Miami and then transfer for a flight to Nassau or to North Eleuthera. I chose the Miami option which would land me into North Eleuthera late tomorrow afternoon. I called Melanie before I checked out of the hotel and left a message on her answering machine to tell her the details of my plans. I promised to call her again when I reached Miami.

I took a taxi to the airport feeling good about myself and excited about returning to the Bahamas.

CHAPTER FIFTEEN

From my window seat on the Twin Air flight to North Eleuthera I had a clear view of the Islands of the Central Bahamas, from Bimini and Cay Cay, to the Berry Islands and the North end of Andros, then along the chain of rocky uninhabited cays that extends northwards from New Providence to Egg Island. I identified Six Shillings Cays, Pimlico Cay, Current Island and Current Cut. As the plane began its descent into the airport, I could see Spanish Wells off to the port side and the small villages of Upper and Lower Bogue and The Bluff off to the right. There were several small boats dotted across the turquoise waters of the shallow banks that surrounded the whole area, and I looked forward to a day, in the not distant future, when mine would be one of them.

There were only a handful of passengers on the flight so we cleared through customs and immigration in record time. It was such a treat to feel warm once again, I felt as though I was returning home. Once I had collected my bags I exited into the bright sunshine and into the waiting arms of my fiancée. It seemed as though we had been apart for a month instead of just a couple of days. Melanie looked prettier and younger here than she did anywhere else. A taxi deposited us at the ferry dock and my bags were transferred to a small boat that soon covered the short distance across the sound to Harbour Island.

I had given a lot of thought to the question of where I should stay while I was in Harbour Island. I was sure that Melanie would insist that I stay with her family in their home, but I had strong reservations as to the correctness of such an idea. I wouldn't feel comfortable sleeping with her under her own roof. I also thought that I should get to know her family in easy stages, maybe dinner one day, an afternoon of boating another day, rather than jumping right in to a twenty four hour a day confrontation. The other consideration was the fact that her father's death had only occurred less than a week ago and I felt that more time should pass before the family had to be placed in a position of accommodating a total stranger. I explained my position to Melanie as diplomatically as I could, I expected her to argue with me, but she understood my concerns and agreed with my logic. She made me promise that we would spend as much time with the family as we could, and I also had to agree to spend some time with her brother on a one on one basis.

"Where do you plan to stay then?" she inquired.

"At Runaway of course" I replied.

"I remember that you told me that if you ever got remarried you would spend your honeymoon there. Is this a honeymoon?"

"Call it a trial run" I laughed.

"You do want me to stay with you?" she asked demurely.

"Naturally, but I don't want you to upset your mother by shacking up with me".

"I told her the situation, everything about us. She understands the situation. She said that she wants to see me happy".

I rented a buggy and drove to the ocean front resort. I booked into a villa that was completely isolated from the main guest house. I had a good reason for not wanting to be in the main hotel building under the continual watch of the staff.

"This is very nice" Melanie said as she tried out the bed "would you like to join me?"

"I have something for you" I said.

"I hoped that you would" she laughed.

"No. I'm serious".

"You're too serious!" she exclaimed.

"You know the situation with my wife. In a few weeks I hope to be single, maybe sooner, but until then we have to remain as we are. I want you to wear this as a sign of my intentions".

I didn't sink down on my knees as she may have expected, but I did withdraw the little ring box from my pocket, open the top, extract the ring and slip it onto her finger.

"I love you, and I want you to be my wife" I said.

We kissed each other passionately and fell backwards onto the bed. I could feel her tears of happiness on my face.

"Oh yes, yes, yes! David I love you so much. You'll never know how much I've wanted to hear those words".

She withdrew herself from my grasp to look at the ring.

"My God, this is exquisite. Look at the size of it. You had this made from one of the stones?" she asked in amazement. "I'll be terrified to wear it. It must be worth a fortune!"

"I had it set in Switzerland by a friend of Bima's. He did a great job".

"But how? You sold all the stones. Didn't you?"

"All except one" I answered.

I wasn't about to tell her that I had secretly pocketed one after they had been weighed. Did it make the gift any less sincere?

"How did you know my size?"

"Annie found out for me".

"Of course, now I remember her getting me to try on rings in that store. So this wasn't a sudden impulse? You've been planning it for a while?"

"Since I first met you" I answered.

She was so excited that she couldn't contain herself. She kissed me again and again while she held her finger out for the light to catch the facets of the ring.

"It's so beautiful. I have to show it to my Mummy, and tell her the news. Come on let's go".

She pulled me outside and jumped into the buggy.

"I'll drive" she shouted.

We drove a short distance to the house where she had been born. I can remember that it was painted bright green and that there was a large tree full of orange flowers in the front, but the rest was a blur in my memory as I was whisked through the house in search of her mother.

Her mother was in the yard painting a picture on a piece of driftwood.

"Mummy, mummy, look! I'm engaged!" she screamed.

She waved the ring under her mother's nose and hugged her.

"My Lord" her Mummy said as she examined the rock that shone from her daughter's finger. "That's the biggest diamond I ever did see!"

She looked up from her seat and clutched my hand.

"You must be David" she said "my daughter has talked about nothing else but you ever since she came home".

"Hello" I said "is it Ok to give my future mother-in-law a hug?"

"Oh my Lord" she cackled "come on then".

Grace Pinder was an elegant woman with high cheekbones and a slender nose that gave her remarkable face the look of an Indian princess. It was obvious that there was no African blood in her veins, she was a direct descendent from the Carib Indians. Her hands, which still held her paint brush, were long and thin like those of an artist. It was easy to see where Melanie had acquired her good looks.

She released me from her tight hug and held me at arms length to study my face, "You have kind eyes" she commented "but your eyes hide your true nature. I can tell that you are part devil and part angel".

"Mummy" exclaimed Melanie "that's rude, to say that. You don't know David. He's all angel!"

"Your mother's right, my wings have been sagging a bit lately".

"I meant no harm" she apologized "I was just commenting on my observation. I trust that I never encounter your devilish side".

There was a wonderful aroma emanating from the kitchen that was making me realize that I had not eaten since early that morning.

Grace must have read my mind as she said, "Can you stay for dinner? I've cooked too much food for just the three of us. Jimmy will be home soon".

"I'd love to stay" I responded "it smells so good".

"It's just pork chops".

A car pulled into the driveway with a squeal; the door banged open and in walked Jimmy Pinder. He was younger than Melanie by two years, so to me he looked like he was barely out of school; he too was a handsome individual with a bright engaging smile.

"This is David" said Melanie.

We shook hands, after which I counted my fingers. This got a big laugh out of Jimmy and got us off on the right track.

"Look" said Melanie as she stuck the engagement ring under his nose, "I'm engaged!"

"Nice" he said "must've cost a fortune".

I discovered that Jimmy had two jobs. He drove a taxi during the day and worked as a bartender at Pink Sands at night. He was also studying to be an accountant through a correspondence course on the internet. He was an intelligent and likeable young man and our conversation during dinner was lively and entertaining, of course that was when we had the chance to talk about something other than the ring and the engagement.

The pork chops were accompanied by beans and rice, macaroni and cheese, cole slaw and Johnny cake. I was to learn during my new life in the Bahamas that the local people liked their food spicy, and if the cook failed to add enough hot pepper, then there was always plenty available on the table as a condiment. To top off a great meal, Grace announced that she had prepared prune whip for desert. I had not tasted prune whip since I was child, when it had been, and still was, one of my favorites. I ate too much of everything.

Jimmy had to get ready for his job at the Hotel. I walked outside with him to his car and asked him if he had a girlfriend that he would like to bring to a small engagement dinner that I was planning for the next evening. He said that he did and that tomorrow was his evening off. I told him where I was staying and that I would arrange for a small dinner party there at about six o'clock.

Melanie had seen us talking outside of the house and had to know what we had been discussing. I told her of my plan and asked her if her mother would agree to join us so soon after her husband's death.

"I wouldn't miss it for the world" she said, after Melanie had invited her and conveyed my concern to her, "my only daughter's engagement is something he would have wanted me to attend. Of course I'll be there".

"Is there anybody else that I should invite?" I asked.

"No" said Grace "if you invite one member of the family you'll have to invite them all, and that little place couldn't hold them all".

"Then it will just be the five of us" I said.

I was wondering whether Melanie was planning to stay with me at Runaway or whether she would stay home with her mother. If there was etiquette about such matters in the Bahamas I wasn't aware of it, so I waited patiently for either Melanie or Grace to broach the subject. If I had had any doubts they were dispelled by Grace as she said to her daughter "You'd better pack an overnight bag with sufficient clothes for a couple of days".

"Yes Mummy" answered Melanie sarcastically "I'm a big girl, ya know, I think I can handle it".

Grace came over to me and whispered jokingly "D'you see what I have to put up with. I'll be glad to be rid of her".

I thanked her for dinner, exchanged another tight hug, collected Melanie's bag from off the floor and stood by the door, ready to leave.

We had had a busy and fruitful day and I was tired and ready to indulge myself in a long and restful sleep, but Melanie had other ideas. One included the use of the bed; however sleeping was not her goal. I was like putty in her hands, well not exactly putty.

"Are you gonna sleep with the ring on your finger?" I asked as I watched her hands at work, "what will you do with it when we go swimming?"

"I dunno. I'll have to find a safe place to hide it".

"You better start looking because first thing in the morning I'm taking a swim in the ocean to clear my head, then I plan to relax around the pool for the rest of the day. These past few days have been rather hectic and my batteries need recharging".

"Tell me where to hide it David, you're smart about such things".

"My suggestion would be to buy a gold chain with a good safety clasp and hang it around your neck, or leave it in the hotel safe".

"I could tape it to my finger".

"With Duct tape I presume?"

"Naturally. I suppose the safe is the answer".

"I never realized that a ring could create such problems. Are you sure that you want to keep it?"

"I'd give up swimming before I gave it back".

In the morning we stopped at the office to put her ring in the safe and to arrange for a table for five for dinner. All the maids, kitchen and front desk staff had to come to see the engagement ring and congratulate her. Melanie was like a kid with a new toy, and I was so happy to see her having the time of her life. I left her with her friends and walked down to the beach. I sat on a chaise under a thatched umbrella and closed my eyes for a moment while I waited for her.

I slept like a baby for most of the morning and would have slept through the afternoon if Melanie hadn't dripped water on me to wake me up. The water was dripping from her wet hair as she knelt over me. It was a pleasant way to awaken, and I thought that maybe I was still dreaming. She collapsed on top of me, pinning me under her wet body. I loved it and didn't struggle or try to push her off, which aggravated her because she was hoping to hear me plead to be left alone. Instead I pulled her closer and thrust my tongue into her ear, and then I reached around and unfastened her bikini top. I slipped the top out from between our bodies and pushed it underneath me. She tried to move me, but she couldn't get any leverage without standing up and exposing herself. She realized that she was in a no win situation and relaxed on top of me in defeat. We stayed glued together for about twenty minutes until my legs felt dead from her weight. I wriggled around to find a different position but could hardly move an inch. I tried to lift her off but discovered that she had her hands clasped together under the chaise and I was helpless.

"I give up" I cried out, "let me up".

She ignored me.

"My legs have gone to sleep" I whimpered.

She continued to ignore me.

"Your mother will be here soon" I commented.

I felt her giggle.

"And Jimmy and his girlfriend. What will she think?" I continued.

She relaxed her grip a touch.

"I'll say, Hi I'm David and I have this creature adhered to me, and I can't get it off. Excuse me if I don't get up!"

She giggled some more, as I continued.

"I went swimming and now this thing is stuck to me like a leach, maybe you could call a doctor or a vet for me to have it removed? I hope that you enjoy your dinner, I wished I could've joined you".

My hands were free but the only parts of Melanie that I could reach were her back, her head and if I really stretched I could get my fingers into her bikini bottom. She must have felt my fingers reaching lower and lower until they were in contact with the string ties that held the flimsy suit together. She realized that I wasn't about to stop and she had to decide if being naked was worth the win. I managed to untie one side with just my two fingers while I worked on the other side. I could feel the tension in her body as she tried to escape from my reach without relaxing her grip around me. I slowly worked my fingers around her until I had a grip on the fabric of her bikini bottom. I pulled as hard as I could and felt the suit come free. She leapt off me and made a mad dash for the ocean. I threw off my clothes and followed her.

I learned something of Melanie's early years as a girl growing up in Harbour Island from her mother and from Jimmy, that night at dinner. They both told stories about her that she would have loved for me not to have heard, but Grace was on a roll and told story after story. When she paused for a moment between stories, Jimmy jumped right in and added one of his. We all laughed together at Melanie's expense, but she was enjoying the attention and holding her own by telling a few stories about her mother and Jimmy.

Jimmy's girlfriend was a waitress at the Harbour Lounge, but was working during the daytime this week, which allowed her to be with us for dinner. She was an attractive girl with big brown eyes and a face that was always wreathed in a smile. She ogled the ring and flashed me a smile that seemed to have a hidden meaning to it. Maybe she was figuring that I was a rich man trying to buy my way into Melanie's affection. That thought had crossed my mind early in our relationship, but I knew now that Melanie's affection was not for sale at any price, it had to be earned.

Although the food and service were outstanding I realized that selecting this place for a dinner party was a mistake. The dining room was better suited to romantic intimate dinners. Later when I confided my thoughts about dinner to Melanie, she disagreed adamantly, saying that they all had a terrific time and had only left early because they had to work the next day and that they also suspected that we would want to be alone.

"Would you like to go dancing?" I asked.

"I'd love to. But I don't want to be out too late".

"Too late for what?"

"I meant that I want to be in bed by midnight".

"And so we shall, my dear" I grinned.

We drove to the Pink Sands Resort where a small group was playing at the Patio Lounge. The stars were shining, the moon was high and full and its light reflecting on the calm ocean; it was a romantic spot, right out of this tropical island's Chamber of Commerce ads.

This was where Jimmy worked and it was evident that the word had been spread throughout the establishment that his sister had become engaged to a rich foreigner. Everyone wanted to take a peek at the 'rock', as I heard it described by one of the staff. Melanie was the envy of all the girls and several of the men expressed their congratulations to me on my catch.

We danced very close all evening and I felt as though I'd finally arrived in heaven; a place that I had always been sure that I would never visit. The music was soft and melodious and the small crowd of dancers moved across the floor in slow motion to the subtle beat of the band.

None of Melanie's family drank alcohol, so I had abstained during dinner as a show of politeness to them, but the cool Anejo and tonic that I had ordered when we had arrived here, tasted like nectar from the Gods. The second one was just as tasty. I caught Melanie admiring her ring after all her well wishers had deserted her; she was turning her hand to catch the moonlight on the ring's facets. She was in another place, miles away. She smiled as she noticed me watching, reached for my hand and leaned in to kiss me.

"I'm so happy David. Its all so perfect, I don't want anything to change".

"I know I feel the same way".

We held on to each other as we walked along the short pathway to the beach where we kicked off our shoes and pushed our toes into the sand. Two beach chairs remained on the beach, left earlier by the day's sun worshippers and we sat and talked for a while about our plans, our dreams and goals and of the life that we were to share.

After a while I looked at my watch and discovered that it was close to midnight and time for 'Cinderella' to go home with her prince.

I awoke at three o'clock as I had planned, slipped out of bed quietly and donned my black running suit. I was taking great care not to wake Melanie as I gathered my flashlight and the few tools that I had secreted away in one of the drawers of the dresser. As I closed the drawer, it emitted a squeak that disturbed Melanie. She opened her eyes for a moment, turned and snuggled back into the bed covers. I waited with bated breath to see if she would fall back into a deep sleep without noticing my absence from the bed. No such luck!

"David?" she asked sleepily, "what are you doing?"

By now she realized that I was dressed and obviously planning on going somewhere.

"Why are you dressed?" she asked curiously.

"I couldn't sleep" I lied "I'm going for a walk on the beach".

"I'll come with you".

"No. You go back to sleep".

She consulted her watch.

"It's three in the morning, David. I'm coming with you".

"I don't want you to. I want to be alone".

"Why? What's wrong? Is it the pork chops?"

"No" I laughed.

"Then what is it? You're up to something. Aren't you?"

I knew that I would have to tell her where I was going, otherwise we would argue all night.

"I'm going to Charlie's house" I told her, "to collect something".

"Collect what?"

"Some papers" I lied again.

"Papers? What papers? David, are you gonna break in?"

"Yes".

"Then I want to come with you".

"You can't. If you were caught with me breaking and entering, you'd be disbarred. I won't let you take that risk".

261

She thought about what I had said for a moment. She understood that I was right.

"You're an officer of the court" I continued "just having knowledge of a crime could be sufficient grounds for your ruination. Now I'm off".

"Please be careful David" she pleaded.

"I'll be back in an hour. Don't worry, I'll be fine".

The night was clear with plenty of moonlight to light my way. I would have preferred a little less. The light from the thousands of stars would have been sufficient. I made my way past the pool and down to the beach and then turned north in the direction of Shangri-La. All was quiet; there was nobody awake anywhere along the way as far as I could determine, there were no lights in any of the hotel windows, and no cleaners working the night shift. I walked the beach unobserved.

Charlie's house was about two hundred yards further along the beach past Pink Sands, where we had danced earlier in the evening. I had made a mental note of the distance during my visit a few weeks ago, I had also made a note of the access to the house from the beach, it consisted of a wooden stairway up the cliffs, and it was this stairway that I was searching for. Every beach front property had a wooden stairway, and as I flashed my flashlight over them, I tried to remember it there had been any distinguishing feature to Charlie's steps.

I did remember talking to Charlie about the fresh water shower that he had installed halfway up his steps for his guests to wash the sand off themselves. As I recalled our conversation, I had commented on the fact that the shower head was gold, or at least gold plated, and I had kidded him about this rather gaudy show of opulence. The light from my flashlight bounced back at me as it reflected off the shiny gold shower head. This was the house.

I scrambled up the stairway to the top of the cliffs, making sure that at no time was I silhouetted against the sky. I stopped for a moment to assess my situation. There was no one around, no dogs, no guards and no alarms. Keeping close to the bushes I made my way past the pool and around the deck to the French doors that led into the game room. I knew that Charlie had an office adjacent to this room and I was sure that I would find what I was looking for in his office. I ran my fingers along the top and sides of the doors, I checked the glass, the hinges and the door handles for any sign of an alarm or motion detector. I was satisfied that the doors were 'clean'. I extracted a screwdriver from my pocket and slipped it between the two doors, one turn and the doors opened. No alarm sounded. I was in. I closed the doors behind me and flipped the lock on the inside to lock the doors. A professional precaution!

I walked quietly through the game room, found the unlocked door to the office, pushed the door open and looked around the office for the most likely place that he would keep his 'papers'.

I opened a drawer in Charlie's desk and hit the jackpot. His check book was sitting on top of his bank statements and other banking papers. I tore one check from his check book and then replaced the book exactly as I had found it.

Next I switched on his computer and waited while it initialized. I typed a note, and then printed it. I deleted the note and switched off the computer, folded the note and placed it together with the blank check in my pocket.

I was about to leave when I saw the outline of someone against the moonlit sky as they walked past the window to the office. I froze! It must be a night watchman, I thought. I listened as he checked every door, turning the door handles to make sure that all the doors were locked. It was his nightly routine. I was thankful that I had had the foresight to have locked the French doors after I had entered. He continued on his inspection tour and was soon out of sight. I waited ten minutes before I opened the doors. I tip toed out of the game room being careful to relock the doors behind me and retraced my steps to the beach.

I was back in the villa in less than an hour. From Melanie's reaction to my reappearance you would have thought that I had been away for a month and in mortal danger. After she realized that I was safe, uninjured and not in any danger, she demanded that I tell her what I was up to.

"I wrote a message to the Royal Bank on Charlie's computer, thanking them for the bridge loan of eight million dollars and advising them that I had enclosed a check for the full amount with the note".

She looked at me with amazement as she digested this information.

"I don't understand" she said.

"You see" I explained "computers are not totally safe. If I had used my own computer and my own printer, there would always be a possibility that the note could have been traced. Even after deleting a note on a computer and emptying the recycle bin, an expert can retrieve almost anything that was ever written on the machine. So I used Charlie's, just to be safe".

"I understand that. But I don't get Charlie's involvement?"

"I've set him up! Just think about the evidence that the police have. Several witnesses saw Charlie's plane land in Spanish Wells on the morning of the robbery. He must be their prime suspect. They know about his dubious past and his police record. I'm going to wire transfer eight million dollars from my account in Switzerland to Charlie's bank account at the Royal Bank in Harbour Island. Then I'm going to write a check from his account to the Royal Bank in Spanish Wells for the same amount. The bank gets their money back, and Charlie is the fall guy!"

It took a few seconds for Melanie to appreciate the brilliance of the plan and to fully grasp the consequences of my actions. When she did, she laughed uncontrollable like a hyena.

"David, my Mummy was right, you are a devil. But what will happen to Charlie?"

"Nothing much, would be my guess. He'll be embarrassed, probably hassled by the police and the bank's inspectors, but since the bank has their money I doubt whether he will be charged with anything more than mischief. He may have to pay a fine; he could be forced to sell his home, if the authorities decide that he is an undesirable character".

"But won't he incriminate you?"

"That will be his first thought, but he'll realize that he will only dig himself in deeper if he admits that he had prior knowledge of the robbery. Sure he knows that I'm the guilty one, but no matter what he tells the police, all the evidence is against him. He'll only make matters worse if he tries to concoct a story to involve me. Charlie has a battery of high priced lawyers on retainer, and for once they will have to earn their keep by making sure that he gets off lightly. After he recovers from his initial shock, he'll be the first to acknowledge the beauty of my subterfuge. He'll go to great lengths to pay me back; it's what I'd do in his position".

"How did you know that he had an account at the Royal Bank?"

"It's the only bank in town. He has a house here and bills to pay. I figured that he must have a local account for his needs here. The one check that I borrowed from him has his account number on it, and I can forge his name quite easily when I make the check to the bank".

"But David, forgery is a major crime".

"Is Charlie gonna bring charges? I don't think so! And the bank won't care because they have the money back. When we were growing up together we spent hours practicing signing each other's names. I can write his signature so well that only a hand writing expert can tell that it's a forgery. A bank teller will have no idea".

"You make it sound like its full proof. Are you sure that you've thought of every possibility?"

"The only problem that remains is the timing of the wire transfer and the issuing of the check to the bank. My guess is that Charlie only ever keeps a small amount of cash in his account, just enough to cover his local bills. When eight million dollars lands in his account there's a possibility that the bank will notify him of such a large deposit. It's doubtful, but the possibility does exist. I have to ensure that the money is withdrawn from his account within minutes of the deposit's arrival. And that is difficult. I can't call the bank to ask if the transfer has arrived and I can't tell the bank in Spanish Wells to wait until the funds are available before depositing their check".

"I might be able to help".

"How?"

"I know the managers of both bank branches; in fact the one in Spanish Wells is a Pinder. Maybe I could present the check to the bank in person and suggest that it be held for deposit pending the arrival of the wire from Switzerland. Then when the money arrives, one bank will notify the other and it will be gone from Charlie's account immediately".

"But how are you supposed to privy to this transaction?"

"As a lawyer I can say that I've been hired anonymously to facilitate this one transaction".

"And you can get away with that?"

"Certainly, lawyers are privileged; I won't have to disclose a thing".

I couldn't find any flaws in her proposal. We rehashed the procedure over and over again trying to find a problem that we had overlooked or a miscalculation that we had made, that could give the bank a reason to suspect that I was involved with Melanie. Her idea would eliminate the risk of Charlie discovering that he had been the unsuspecting recipient of eight million dollars, and him removing the money before the bank had processed their check. The last thing I wanted was for Charlie to be the beneficiary of the money.

"You'll have to fabricate a story to relay to the bank".

"I'll tell them that I received a call from Charlie's attorney asking me to deliver an envelope to the bank. I'll say that my instructions are to advise them that the funds to cover the amount of the check have been wired from a foreign bank, and should arrive within a few hours"

"Are you sure that you want to do this?"

"Absolutely, when will you make the call to Switzerland?" she asked.

"I can call right now" I replied.

"Then what are you waiting for?" she urged "make the call".

I placed the call to the Guardian Bank, identified myself to the computer and was cleared through to Mister George. I relayed Charlie's account number to him and verified that the amount of the transfer was for eight million dollars. He read back the account number for my confirmation and advised me that the money should be available in the account within a few hours. I thanked him and hung up.

"It's done" I said as I replaced the telephone to its cradle, "he said it should only take an hour or two".

"We'll ride over on the BoHengy at eleven".

"What would I do without you? Bert told me not to let you get away".

"He did? So you're only marrying me to satisfy Bert?"

"That's the only reason; I'd never be able to show my face in the Rose and Crown again, if I didn't. And then I'd miss their rendition of 'Hold That Tiger'. By the way does your Mummy know that story?"

"No, and don't you tell her".

"As if I would" I teased.

CHAPTER SIXTEEN

While Melanie was busy putting on her lawyer's 'uniform' in preparation for her visit to the bank, I took the time to practice my Charles Wolfsen signature. After a dozen attempts I was satisfied enough with the result to place the signature on the bottom of the check that I had made payable to the Royal Bank in the amount of eight million dollars. I decided not to sign the thank-you note. I placed the check and the note in a plain white envelope ready for Melanie to deliver to the bank.

I had convinced Melanie to stay in Spanish Wells for at least a day or two for a couple of reasons. Firstly, the ferry wouldn't be returning until the next day, secondly I wanted to stick around until the bank confirmed that it had received the money and thirdly, I wanted to be sure that Spanish Wells was the place in which I intended to settle, and that decision now included Melanie.

I checked out of Runaway, collected Melanie and our two small bags and hurried to the Government dock where the BoHengy was already boarding for the short trip to Spanish Wells.

As the ferry slowed to enter the channel that led into the town, I was overcome by a strange feeling of deja vu. It was foolish for me to consider this place as home, but the familiar waterfront and the coulouful buildings stirred my memory and made me feel as though I belonged.

I rented a buggy from Abner's for Melanie's trip to the bank and told her that I would wait at the Anchor Café while she conducted her business. I wished her the best, kissed her goodbye and with my fingers crossed for good luck, I sauntered along the dock to pass the time.

The 'coffee club' members were congregated in their usual hang out by the fuel dock, arguing about the state of the countries affairs and having a heated debate about the best remedy for the problems that existed. I could hear their loud accented voices rising in volume as they tried to express their points of view on every topic under the sun; it was obvious that they held to the conviction that by talking louder and louder they could drown out any opposing ideas. I poked my nose into the Marine store where there was usually a collection of local fishermen complaining about the weather, or the poachers, or the price of fuel or some other problem that they faced in their daily lives.

I continued on my stroll to the eastern most point of the island past many of the old original wooden houses that had withstood many hurricanes and numerous floods. Some of the houses had been purchased by wealthy Americans and were undergoing considerable renovations; it was clear that others had discovered this ideal island and were making it their winter get away or their retirement haven. From this point it was easy to see across the water to Gun Point and the small community that dotted the slopes of the small hills between the Point and Ridley Head.

I turned the corner and started to head west, I passed the 'private' school, the People's Church, then turned south and walked between the blue painted buildings that comprised Ronald's Service Center. It was here that you could buy lumber, building materials, paint supplies and household hardware, while across the road was the place where the tons and tons of crawfish were processed.

By the time I entered the Anchor Café I was ready for a cold beer, but I knew that I'd have to settle for iced tea instead. I found an empty table in the corner and as I settled into my seat one of the four or five attractive waitresses that worked there appeared at my shoulder with pad and pencil in hand to take my order. I ordered a jumbo iced tea while I waited for Melanie.

I could hear intermittent pounding coming from the kitchen which meant that one of the lunch time customers had ordered cracked conch.

Melanie had now been at the bank for more than an hour. Had something gone wrong? To deliver an envelope and a few simple instructions should have only taken ten minutes or so. I was getting worried. I was on the point of leaving the café to go and find her, when she burst through the door. She saw me at a table and hurried over to join me.

"I was getting worried" I said as she ordered a large iced tea from our waitress "was there a problem?"

"No, it was a piece of cake" she laughed "it's done. They have the money. It arrived while I was at the bank".

"Tell me everything" I said with a big sigh of relief.

"When I walked in to the manager's office, the first thing he said was that he was sorry to hear about my father's passing. I knew that he was family. I told him that I was there to deliver an envelope, which I handed to him while I recounted the instructions that had supposedly been passed to me via Charlie's attorney.

He opened the envelope studied the check and read the note. His face went pale as the impact of the envelope's contents registered in his brain. He was literally speechless. He reread the note before uttering 'bridge loan indeed. What a nerve'. He asked me how I had come to have the envelope and I told him that I had been contacted by an attorney from England by telephone, and that the envelope had been delivered to me. He called his superior in Nassau to relay the information, and then he called the manager in the Harbour Island branch to verify the authenticity of Charlie's account number. While he was on the call the money arrived in the account and was immediately put on hold".

"You don't think that he was suspicious?"

"Not at all. He was almost jumping for joy. We certainly made his day".

"Let's hope that all the bank's officials will have the same reaction".

"You must feel relieved".

"Relieved? I don't know if that's the right word. I know that I'm eight million dollars poorer!"

"I'd love to be there when Charlie receives the news. Do you think that he'll call you?"

"Oh yes. I've no doubt that he will".

I decided to have the cracked conch for lunch; I just wanted to hear more of the rhythmic pounding, while Melanie ordered a double whopper with cheese and fries. She is such a gourmet, but I love her anyway.

"I need to make a phone call" she said.

"I think that it's Ok to use the phone that's on the counter".

She walked to the counter and dialed a number, talked for a moment and returned to the table.

"I think that I've found the perfect location for my office" she stated without batting an eye.

"Your what?"

"My office, you suggested that this would be the best place to hang my shingle".

"I know, but I wasn't sure that you agreed with me. I was afraid to press the point as I thought you might be leaning towards somewhere close to home".

"I think you're right. This place needs a good lawyer. There's a lot happening here".

"Where is it?" I inquired.

"I'll show you after lunch. The landlord is meeting us there".

The new office was located over the bank. The landlord opened the doors to let us wander through its spacious interior. It was a very nice apartment that had been rented for several years to the local Customs official, but a change in the Government's plans had forced the tenant to vacate the place. It was a perfect location, and had enormous potential. Melanie had made up her mind and gave the landlord a check for the first month's rent.

Outside and in our rented buggy I hugged her close and kissed her very tenderly because I knew that she had decided on locating in Spanish Wells to conform to my wishes, and even though the office was just about perfect and she did agree that this was a good idea, her heart was really closer to home with her family and friends.

"Add another Pinder to the phone book" I joked "what will you put on your shingle M. Pinder or Melanie Pinder?"

"Melanie" she answered "I think there's already another attorney named M. Pinder".

We drove around town in the buggy from one end of the island to the other. We acknowledged the gestures of friendship from the passing motorists with a wave and I marveled at the way everyone took time to be friendly. The school day was over and the mothers were out in force to pick up their clone-like offspring; there was an actual traffic tie up outside of the school, it was the most traffic that I had seen at one time, but no one cursed or complained. Life in Spanish Wells would seem to be boring to many people, but for me it offered a way of life that in most parts of the world had disappeared with the advent of terrorism, violence, hysteria, dishonesty and disenchantment.

I thought about the weeks that had taken me on an adventure that I would never forget and about the girl I was with in the golf cart who would one day soon, become my wife. If there was a lesson to be learned from this experience then it would have to be in my future answer to that familiar question that would be posed to me again and again.

"Is there anything you can't do?"

And my new answer would be.

"Skate backwards; play the violin; keep a secret!"

About the Author

Derek Hawkins was born and raised in London where he attended London University before emigrating to Canada. He has traveled extensively throughout the Bahamas and the world, finally settling down in Spanish Wells to live and operate a fish farm and fish hatchery.

Printed in the United States
19799LVS00001B/154-261